LEVEL 4 Supplemental

ULTIMATE MUSIC THEORY

By Glory St. Germain ARCT RMT MYCC UMTC &
Shelagh McKibbon-U'Ren RMT UMTC

The LEVEL 4 Supplemental Workbook is designed to be completed with the Basic Rudiments Workbook.

GSG MUSIC

Enriching Lives Through Music Education

ISBN: 978-1-927641-45-3

# The Ultimate Music Theory™ Program

The Ultimate Music Theory™ Program lays the foundation of music theory education.

The focus of the Ultimate Music Theory Program is to simplify complex concepts and show the relativity of these concepts with practical application. This program is designed to help teachers and students discover the excitement and benefits of a sound music theory education.

The Ultimate Music Theory Program is based on a proven approach to the study of music theory that follows the *"must have"* Learning Principles to develop effective learning for all learning styles.

The Ultimate Music Theory™ Program and Supplemental Workbooks help students prepare for nationally recognized theory examinations including the Royal Conservatory of Music.

GSG MUSIC

Library and Archives Canada Cataloguing in Publication
UMT Supplemental Series / Glory St. Germain and Shelagh McKibbon-U'Ren

Gloryland Publishing - UMT Supplemental Workbook and Answer Book Series:

GP-SPL	ISBN: 978-1-927641-41-5	UMT Supplemental Prep Level
GP-SL1	ISBN: 978-1-927641-42-2	UMT Supplemental Level 1
GP-SL2	ISBN: 978-1-927641-43-9	UMT Supplemental Level 2
GP-SL3	ISBN: 978-1-927641-44-6	UMT Supplemental Level 3
GP-SL4	ISBN: 978-1-927641-45-3	UMT Supplemental Level 4
GP-SL5	ISBN: 978-1-927641-46-0	UMT Supplemental Level 5
GP-SL6	ISBN: 978-1-927641-47-7	UMT Supplemental Level 6
GP-SL7	ISBN: 978-1-927641-48-4	UMT Supplemental Level 7
GP-SL8	ISBN: 978-1-927641-49-1	UMT Supplemental Level 8
GP-SCL	ISBN: 978-1-927641-50-7	UMT Supplemental Complete Level
GP-SPLA	ISBN: 978-1-927641-51-4	UMT Supplemental Prep Level Answer Book
GP-SL1A	ISBN: 978-1-927641-52-1	UMT Supplemental Level 1 Answer Book
GP-SL2A	ISBN: 978-1-927641-53-8	UMT Supplemental Level 2 Answer Book
GP-SL3A	ISBN: 978-1-927641-54-5	UMT Supplemental Level 3 Answer Book
GP-SL4A	ISBN: 978-1-927641-55-2	UMT Supplemental Level 4 Answer Book
GP-SL5A	ISBN: 978-1-927641-56-9	UMT Supplemental Level 5 Answer Book
GP-SL6A	ISBN: 978-1-927641-57-6	UMT Supplemental Level 6 Answer Book
GP-SL7A	ISBN: 978-1-927641-58-3	UMT Supplemental Level 7 Answer Book
GP-SL8A	ISBN: 978-1-927641-59-0	UMT Supplemental Level 8 Answer Book
GP-SCLA	ISBN: 978-1-927641-60-6	UMT Supplemental Complete Level Answer Book

Respect Copyright - Copyright 2017 Gloryland Publishing

All rights reserved. No part of this publication may be reproduced or transmitted in any form or by any means, electronic or mechanical, including photocopying, recording, or any information storage and retrieval system, without permission in writing from the author/publisher.

* Resources - An annotated list is available at UltimateMusicTheory.com under Free Resources.

Ultimate Music Theory

LEVEL 4 Supplemental

Table of Contents

Ultimate Music Theory	The Story of UMT... Meet So-La & Ti-Do	4
Comparison Chart	Level 4	6
Terms and Half Steps	Signs for String Instruments and Chromatic Scales	8
Circle of Fifths	Major Scales and Scale Degrees	10
Circle of Fifths	Minor Scales and Scale Degrees	14
Minor Scales	Natural minor scales, Degrees and Key Signatures	15
Minor Scales	Harmonic minor scales, Degrees and Key Signatures	18
Minor Scales	Melodic minor scales, Degrees and Key Signatures	21
Same Word	Different Concept and Interval Review	24
Tonic Triads	Functional & Root/Quality Chord Symbols	26
Subdominant Triads	Functional & Root/Quality Chord Symbols	28
Dominant Triads	Functional & Root/Quality Chord Symbols	30
Chord Symbols	Review - Functional & Root/Quality Chord Symbols	32
Conducting	Duple, Triple & Quadruple Time; Bar Line & Rest Reviews	34
Transposition	Transposing One Octave - Same Clef or Change of Clef	38
Analysis of Melody	Melodic Motive, Melodic Phrase - Same, Similar or Different	40
Composition	Analysis of Motive, Phrase and Section	42
Composition	Four Measure Melody - Ending on Stable Scale Degrees	44
ICE & Analysis	Imagine, Compose, Explore & Sight Reading - Funny Ferret	46
Orchestra Family	Instruments and Sections - Organize the Orchestra	48
Music Appreciation	Musical Instruments & Voice - Range Chart & Tone Color	50
Music History	Benjamin Britten - Young Person's Guide to the Orchestra	52
Music History	Pyotr Tchaikovsky - The Nutcracker	54
Musical Instruments	Coloring the Orchestra Families	56
Theory Exam	Level 4	57
Certificate	Completion of Level 4	64

Score: **60 - 69** Pass; **70 - 79** Honors; **80 - 89** First Class Honors; **90 - 100** First Class Honors with Distinction

Ultimate Music Theory: *The Way to Score Success!*

Workbooks, Exams, Answers, Online Courses, App & More!

A Proven Step-by-Step System to Learn Theory Faster - from Beginner to Advanced.

Innovative techniques designed to develop a complete understanding of music theory, to enhance sight reading, ear training, creativity, composition and musical expression.

All UMT Series have matching Answer Books!

The UMT Rudiments Series - Beginner A, Beginner B, Beginner C, Prep 1, Prep 2, Basic, Intermediate, Advanced & Complete (All-In-One)

♪ 12 Lessons, Review Tests, and a Final Exam to develop confidence
♪ Music Theory Guide & Chart for fast and easy reference of theory concepts
♪ 80 Flashcards for fun drills to dramatically increase retention & comprehension

Rudiments Exam Series - Preparatory, Basic, Intermediate & Advanced

♪ 8 Exams plus UMT Tips on How to Score 100% on Theory Exams

Each Rudiments Workbook correlates to a Supplemental Workbook.

The UMT Supplemental Series - Prep Level, Level 1, Level 2, Level 3, Level 4, Level 5, Level 6, Level 7, Level 8 & Complete (All-In-One) Level

♪ Form & Analysis and Music History - Composers, Eras & Musical Styles
♪ Melody Writing using ICE - Imagine, Compose & Explore
♪ 12 Lessons, Review Tests, Final Exam and 80 Flashcards for quick study

Supplemental Exam Series - Level 5, Level 6, Level 7 & Level 8

♪ 8 Exams to successfully prepare for nationally recognized Theory Exams

UMT Online Courses, Music Theory App & More

♪ UMT Certification Course, Teachers Membership & Elite Educator Program
♪ Ultimate Music Theory App correlates to the Rudiments Workbooks
♪ Free Resources - Teachers Guide, Music Theory Blogs, videos & downloads

Go To: UltimateMusicTheory.com

At Ultimate Music Theory we are passionate about helping teachers and students experience the joy of teaching and learning music by creating the most effective music theory materials on the planet!

Introducing the Ultimate Music Theory Family!

So-La

Meet So-La! So-La loves to sing and dance.

She is expressive, creative and loves to tell stories through music!

So-La feels music in her heart. She loves to teach, compose and perform.

Ti-Do

Meet Ti-Do! Ti-Do loves to count and march.

He is rhythmic, consistent and loves the rules of music theory!

Ti-Do feels music in his hands and feet. He loves to analyze, share tips and conduct.

So-La & Ti-Do will guide you through Mastering Music Theory!

Enriching Lives Through Music Education

The Ultimate Music Theory™ Comparison Chart to the 2016 Royal Conservatory of Music Theory Syllabus.
Level 4

The Ultimate Music Theory™ Rudiments Workbooks, Supplemental Workbooks and Exams prepare students for successful completion of the Royal Conservatory of Music Theory Levels.

UMT Basic Rudiments Workbook plus the LEVEL 4 Supplemental Workbook = RCM Theory Level 4.
♪ Note: Additional completion of the LEVEL 5 Supplemental Workbook = RCM Theory Level 5.

RCM Level 4 Theory Concept	Ultimate Music Theory Basic Workbook
Required Keys: - Up to 3 sharps and 3 flats C, G, D, A, F, B-flat, E-flat Major a, e, b, f-sharp, d, g, c minor	**Keys Covered:** - Up to 4 sharps and 4 flats C, G, D, A, E, F, B-flat, E-flat, A-flat Major a, e, b, f-sharp, c-sharp, d, g, c, f minor * Workbook Pages - Circle of Fifths - Up to 3 sharps and 3 flats
Pitch and Notation: - Transposition up/down one octave, including change of clef	**Pitch and Notation Covered:** - Transposition up/down one octave, including change of clef - Rewriting a melody at the same pitch in the alternate clef * Workbook Page - Transposition - One Octave - Change of Clef * Workbook Page - Transposition - Same Clef or Change of Clef
Rhythm and Meter - Time Signatures: 2/4, 3/4, 4/4, 2/8, 3/8, 4/8 - bar lines, notes and rests - Triplets (eighth notes)	**Rhythm and Meter Covered** - Time Signatures: All Simple Time Signatures (2/2, 3/2, 4/2, 2/4, 3/4, 4/4, 2/8, 3/8, 4/8); bar lines, notes and rests * Workbook Pages - Conducting Patterns in Simple Time (Duple, Triple and Quadruple) - Triplets (quarter notes, eighth notes, sixteenth notes)
Intervals - Melodic and Harmonic intervals (Major, minor and Perfect) up to an octave (using Key Signatures or Accidentals) above the Tonic of the required Major keys only	**Intervals Covered** - Writing and Identifying - Melodic and Harmonic intervals (Major, minor and Perfect) up to an octave (using Key Signatures or Accidentals) above the Tonic of Major Keys with up to 4 sharps/4 flats * Workbook Pages - Interval Review - (Perfect, Major and minor)
Scales and Scale Degree Names - Scales using Key Signatures and/or Accidentals: Major: C, G, D, A, F, B-flat, E-flat; Minor (natural, harmonic and melodic): a, e, b, f-sharp, d, g, c - Scale Degree Names: Tonic, Subdominant, Dominant, Leading Tone and Subtonic	**Scales and Scale Degree Names Covered** - Scales using Key Signatures and/or Accidentals: Major: C, G, D, A, E, F, B-flat, E-flat, A-flat; Minor (natural, harmonic and melodic): a, e, b, f-sharp, c-sharp, d, g, c, f - Scale Degree Names: Tonic, Subdominant, Dominant * Workbook Pages - Scale Degree Names: Lower Tonic, Mediant, Subdominant, Dominant, Leading Tone, Upper Tonic and Subtonic * Workbook Pages - Chromatic Scale - Half Steps
Chords - Tonic, Subdominant and Dominant Triads of required keys in Root Position (solid/blocked or broken form) - Functional Chord Symbols (I, i, IV, iv, V) - Root/Quality Chord Symbols (ex. C, Am)	**Chords Covered** - Tonic, Subdominant and Dominant Triads of required keys in Root Position (solid/blocked or broken form) written using Key Signatures or Accidentals - Triad Degrees (I, i, IV, iv, V) * Workbook Pages - Review of Functional Chord Symbols (Triad Degrees) - Tonic, Subdominant and Dominant Triads in Major and Relative minor keys (Solid/blocked and broken) * Workbook Pages - Root/Quality Chord Symbols - Tonic, Subdominant and Dominant Triads in Major and Relative minor keys

* Supplemental Workbook Pages - New concepts introduced in the 2016 RCM Theory Syllabus.

RCM Level 4 Theory Concept (Continued)

Analysis
- Identification of concepts from this level and the previous levels within short music examples
- Identification of sections (A and B) within a short piece

Melody and Composition
- Composition of a 4-measure melody in a Major Key using steps, skips and leaps (between notes of the Tonic and Dominant triads) and ending on stable scale degree $\hat{1}$ or $\hat{3}$

Musical Terms and Signs
- Tempo, Dynamics and Articulation

Music History/Appreciation
- Families of Orchestral Instruments

- The Young Person's Guide to the Orchestra by Benjamin Britten

- The Nutcracker (by Pyotr Il'yich Tchaikovsky)
   - Waltz of the Flowers
   - Dance of the Sugar Plum Fairy

Examination
(No Level 4 Theory Exam)

Ultimate Music Theory Basic Workbook (Continued)

Analysis Covered
* Workbook Pages - Analysis of Melody - Identification of concepts from this level and the previous levels within short music examples
* Workbook Pages - Analysis of Composition - Identification of sections (A and B) within a short piece

Melody and Composition Covered
* Workbook Pages - Composition of a four measure melody in a Major Key using repetition, steps, skips and leaps (between notes of the Tonic and Dominant triads) and ending on stable scale degree $\hat{1}$ or $\hat{3}$
Composition elements of music - Melody, Rhythm and Harmony

Musical Terms and Signs Covered
* Workbook Pages - Musical Terms and Signs
* Workbook Page Bonus - Analysis and Sight Reading

Music History/Appreciation Covered
* Workbook Pages - Review of Families of Orchestral Instruments (previously introduced in UMT Level 1 Supplemental Workbook)
* Workbook Pages - Instrumental range and tone color

* Workbook Pages - The Young Person's Guide to the Orchestra by Benjamin Britten
Listening Focus: Families and instruments used; range and color

* Workbook Pages - Life and Music of Pyotr Il'yich Tchaikovsky
* Workbook Pages - The Nutcracker (by Pyotr Il'yich Tchaikovsky)
   - Waltz of the Flowers
   - Dance of the Sugar Plum Fairy
Listening Focus: Families and instruments used; range and color

Review Tests & Final Exam
- 12 Accumulative Review Tests (1 with each of the 12 Lessons)
* UMT LEVEL 4 THEORY EXAM

"The creative process is like music which takes root with extraordinary force and rapidity." - Tchaikovsky

---

UltimateMusicTheoryApp.com - Over 7000 Flashcards including audio! 6 Subjects: Beginner - Prep, Basic, Intermediate, Advanced, Ear Training & Music Trivia (including History).

Basic Music Theory App Subject - Use with the Basic Rudiments Workbook

12 Decks - 1,329 Cards - See, hear and identify notes, intervals, scales, triads and musical terms. Learn notation, the Circle of Fifths, Key Signatures, Simple Time and more!

1 - Music Notation - Notes & Rests

2 - Accidentals - Sharp, Flat & Natural

3 - Enharmonic Equivalents, Tones

4 - Circle of Fifths, Major keys & Major scales

5 - Intervals - Perfect, Major and minor

6 - Circle of Fifths, minor keys & minor scales

7 - Triads - Major and minor

8 - Simple Time - Double, Triple and Quadruple

9 - Identifying the Key of a Melody (Maj/min)

10 - Transposition - Up or Down One Octave

11 - Analysis - Musical Compositions

12 - Musical Terms, Definitions and Signs

MUSICAL TERMS and SIGNS (Use after Basic Rudiments Page 34)

Musical Terms and Signs indicate dynamics, articulation, tempo (such as *Vivace* meaning lively, brisk), etc. Terms and signs may also be used for stringed instruments to indicate how to bow or pluck the strings.

Musical Terms and Signs for string instruments indicate specific performance details.

So-La Says: The two usual ways of playing a string instrument are: bowed or plucked.

pizzicato (pizz.) means to pluck the strings.

arco means to resume bowing after a *pizzicato* passage.

⸴ **breath mark** means take a breath, and/or a slight pause or lift.

⊓ **down bow** means on a bowed string instrument, play the note while drawing the bow downward.

V **up bow** means on a bowed string instrument, play the note while drawing the bow upward.

This excerpt (passage or segment) from "The Happy Farmer" by Robert Schumann is notated for violin.

This excerpt (passage or segment) from "The Happy Farmer" by Robert Schumann is notated for piano.

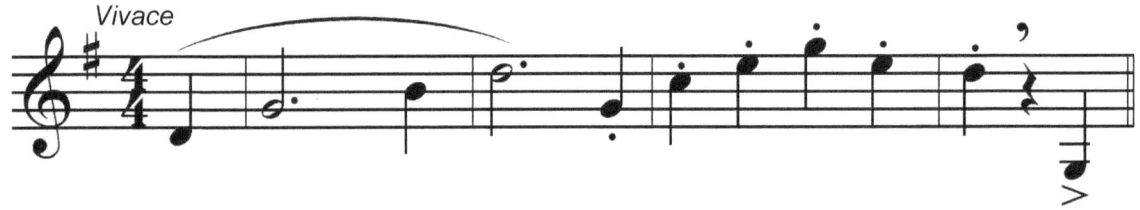

1. Draw a line to match the Musical Term or Sign with the correct definition.

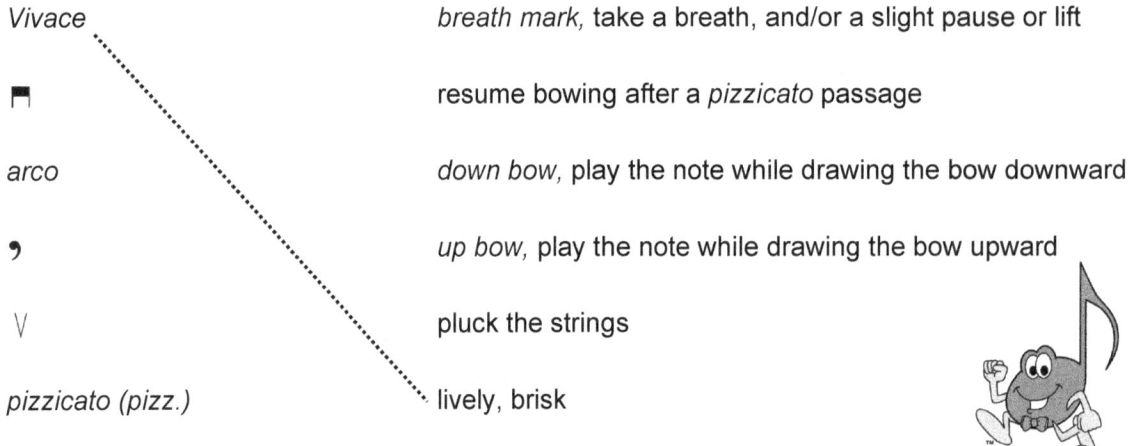

Vivace	*breath mark,* take a breath, and/or a slight pause or lift
⊓	resume bowing after a *pizzicato* passage
arco	*down bow,* play the note while drawing the bow downward
⸴	*up bow,* play the note while drawing the bow upward
V	pluck the strings
pizzicato (pizz.)	lively, brisk

CHROMATIC SCALE - HALF STEPS (Use after Basic Rudiments Page 34)

A **Half Step** may be written as Chromatic (SAME letter name) or Diatonic (DIFFERENT letter name). A scale that moves by half steps (written with both chromatic and diatonic half steps) is called a **Chromatic scale**.

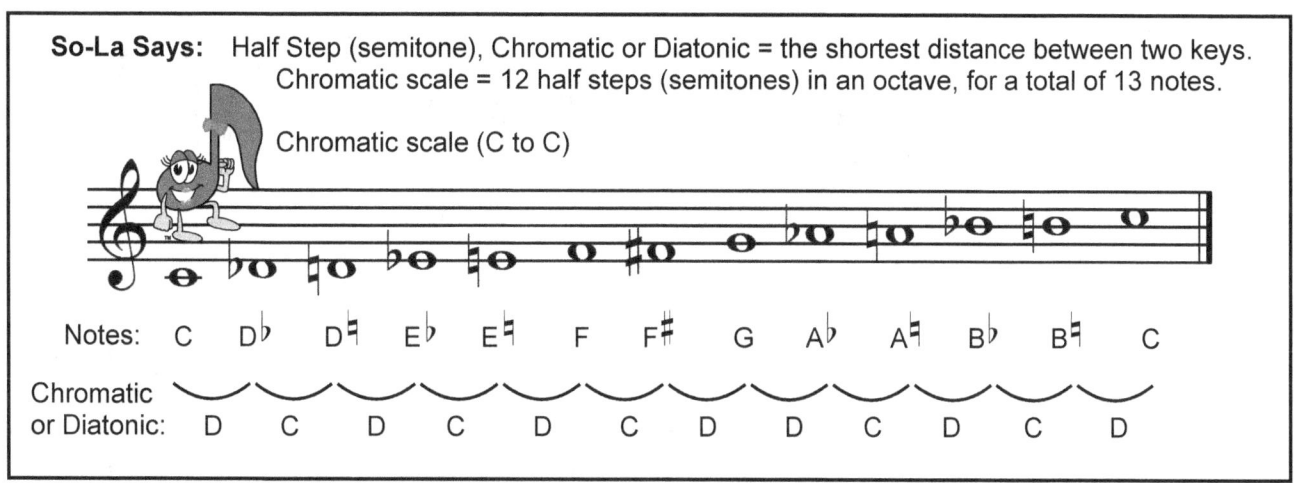

1. Name the notes of the Chromatic scale (A to A). Identify each half step as: **C** - Chromatic or **D** - Diatonic. Draw a line from each note to the corresponding key on the keyboard (at the correct pitch).

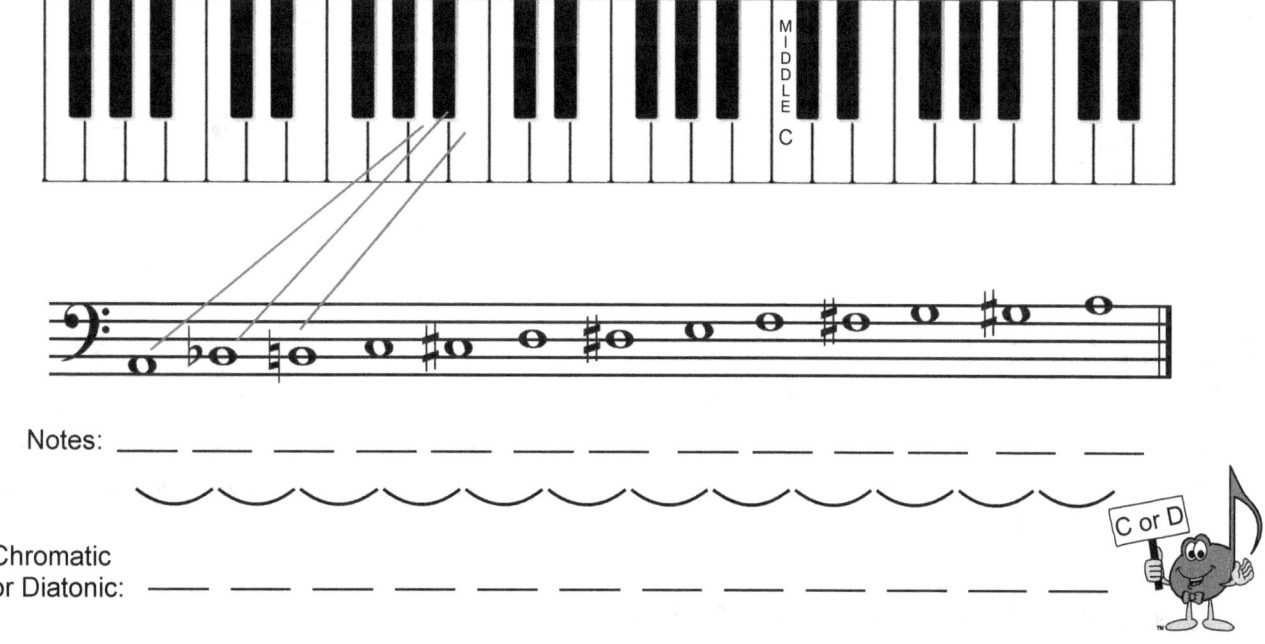

2. Add accidentals where necessary to complete the Chromatic scale (G to G). Name the notes.

Notes: ___ ___ ___ ___ ___ ___ ___ ___ ___ ___ ___ ___ ___

CIRCLE OF FIFTHS - MAJOR KEY SIGNATURES (Use after Basic Rudiments Page 48)

The Circle of Fifths is a map of the Major and minor Key Signatures. It identifies the number of flats and sharps found in each key. The distance from one key to the next key around the Circle of Fifths is a fifth. Each fifth is 5 letter names and 7 half steps (semitones).

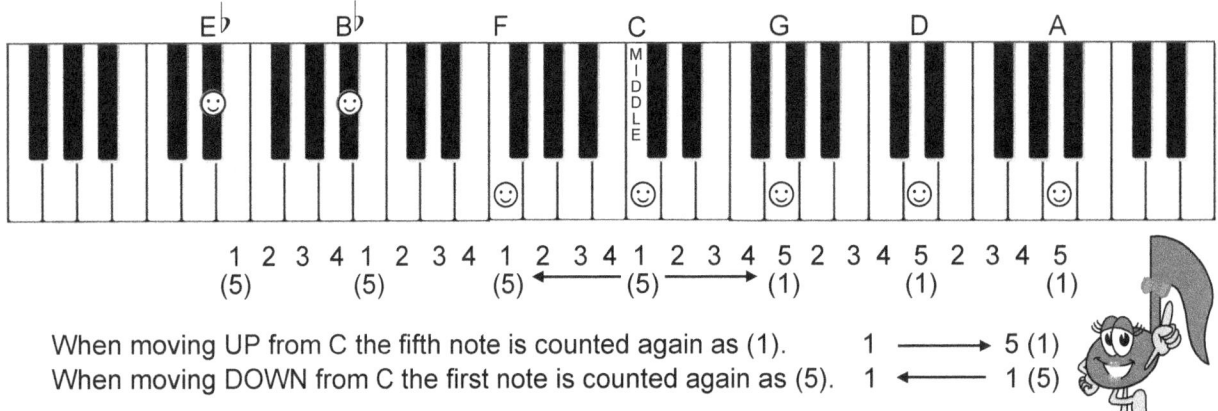

When moving UP from C the fifth note is counted again as (1).   1 ⟶ 5 (1)
When moving DOWN from C the first note is counted again as (5).   1 ⟵ 1 (5)

So-La Says: The Circle of Fifths maps out the Major Keys up to and including 3 sharps and 3 flats.

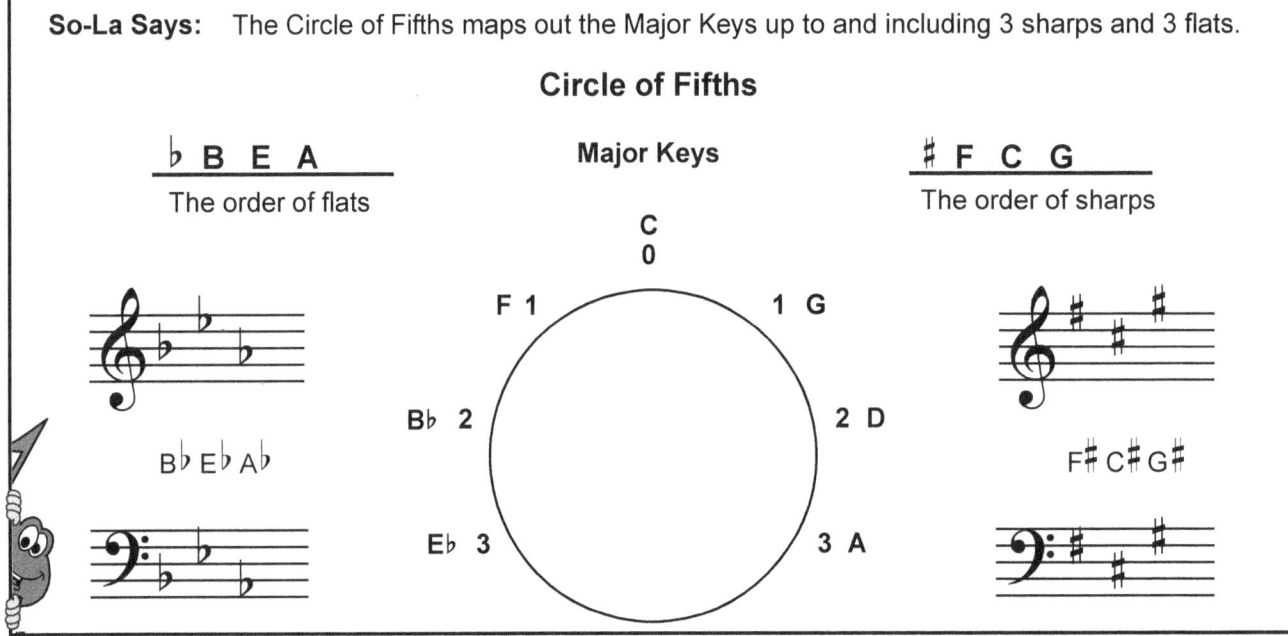

♪ **Ti-Do Tip:** A sharp or flat in a Key Signature applies to all notes, on the staff or using ledger lines, with that letter name.

1. a) Name the notes.
   b) Name the Major key for the following Key Signatures.

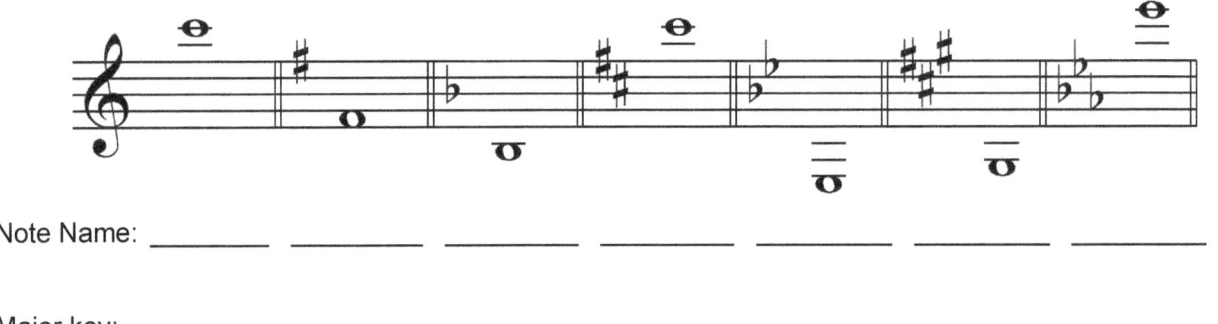

Note Name: _____ _____ _____ _____ _____ _____ _____

Major key: _____ _____ _____ _____ _____ _____ _____

UltimateMusicTheory.com © Copyright 2017 Gloryland Publishing. All Rights Reserved.

MAJOR SCALES and SCALE DEGREES (Use after Basic Rudiments Page 48)

A **Major scale** is a series of 8 notes in a specific pattern:

$\hat{1}$ whole step $\hat{2}$ whole step $\hat{3}$ half step $\hat{4}$ whole step $\hat{5}$ whole step $\hat{6}$ whole step $\hat{7}$ half step $\hat{8}$ ($\hat{1}$).

Scale Degree Numbers are numbers with a circumflex, caret sign or hat (^) written above the number. Scale Degree Numbers are written below the notes of a scale.

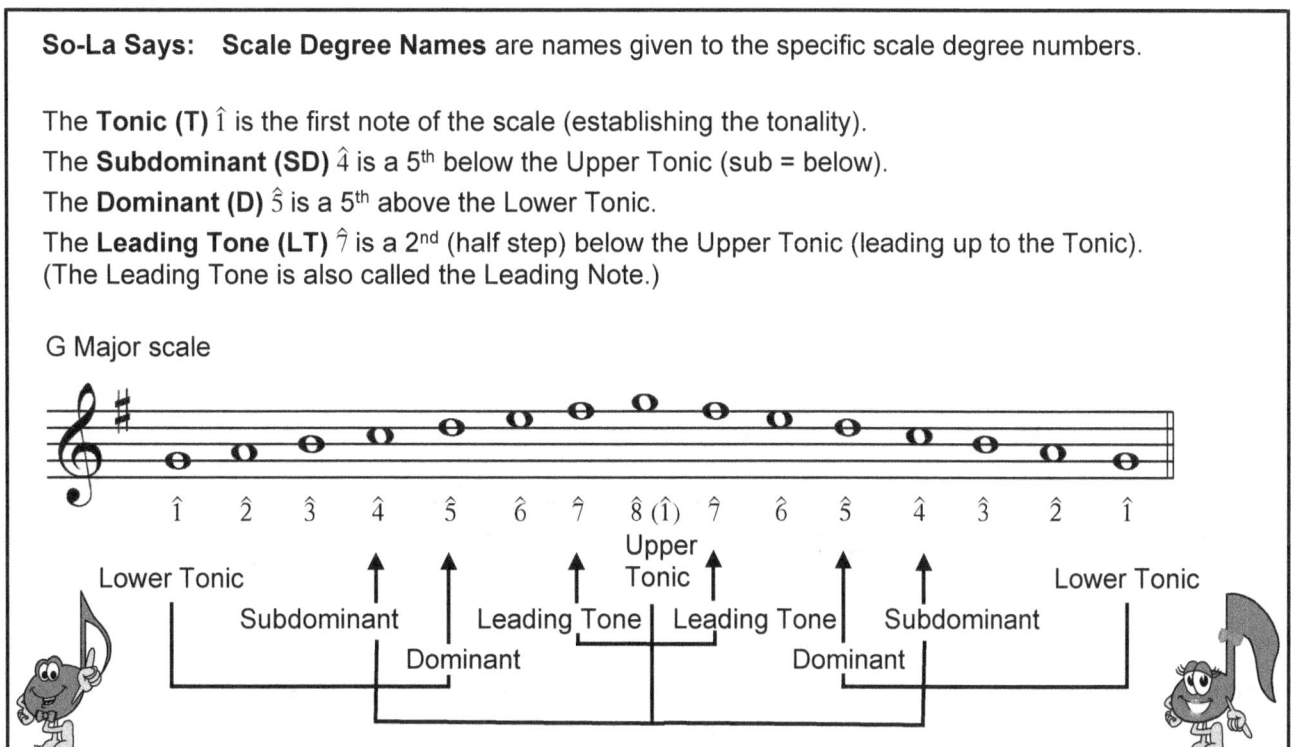

So-La Says: Scale Degree Names are names given to the specific scale degree numbers.

The **Tonic (T)** $\hat{1}$ is the first note of the scale (establishing the tonality).
The **Subdominant (SD)** $\hat{4}$ is a 5th below the Upper Tonic (sub = below).
The **Dominant (D)** $\hat{5}$ is a 5th above the Lower Tonic.
The **Leading Tone (LT)** $\hat{7}$ is a 2nd (half step) below the Upper Tonic (leading up to the Tonic).
(The Leading Tone is also called the Leading Note.)

G Major scale

♪ **Ti-Do Tip:** A Whole Step is also called a Whole Tone; a Half Step is also called a Semitone.

1. a) Write the Scale Degree Numbers below each note.
   b) Below each scale, label each Tonic (T), Subdominant (SD), Dominant (D) and Leading Tone (LT).

E♭ Major scale

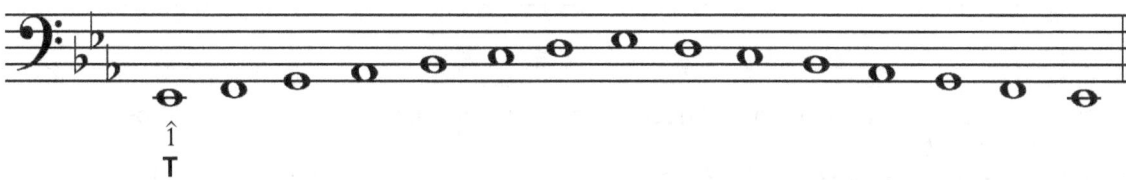

A Major scale

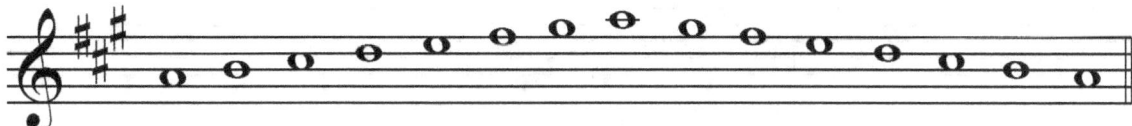

MAJOR SCALES and SCALE DEGREES USING ACCIDENTALS (Use after Basic Rudiments Page 53)

Major Scale Patterns are used to identify the accidentals found in each Major scale.

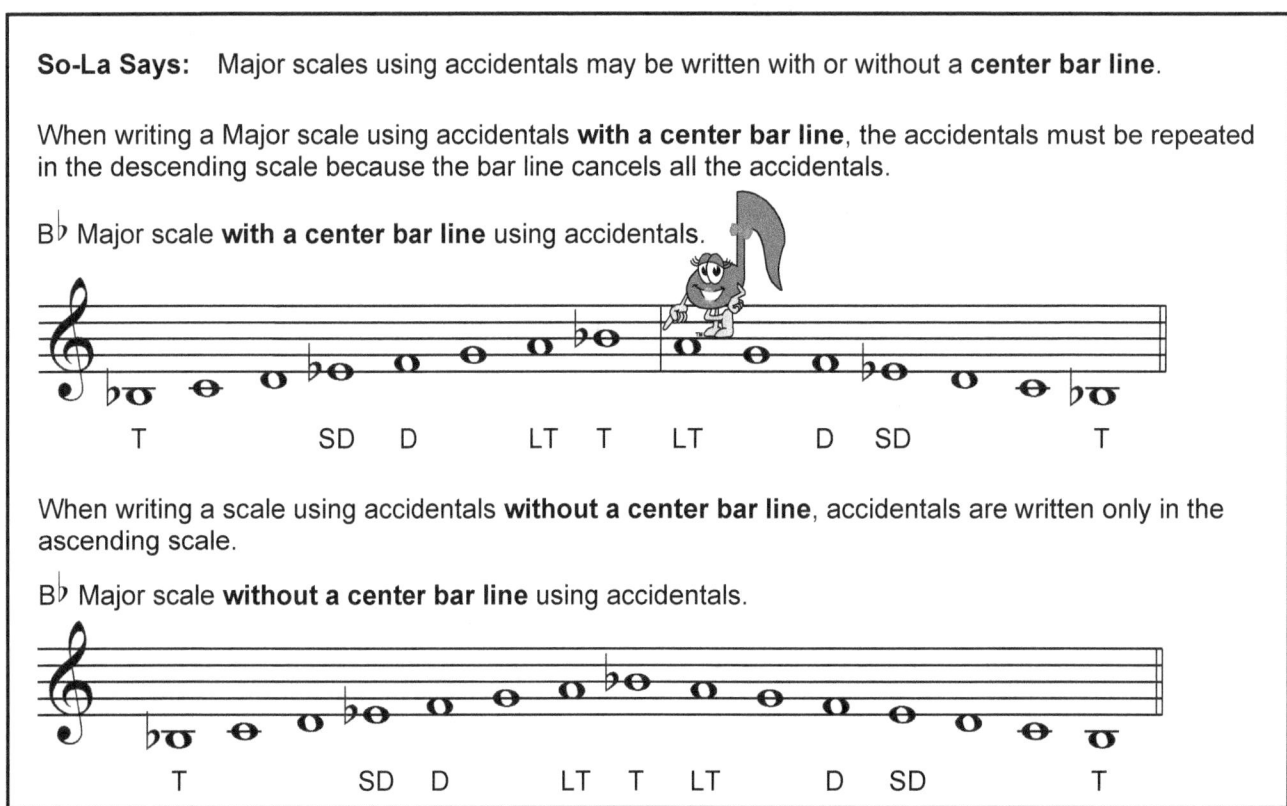

♪ **Ti-Do Tip:** An accidental applies to the notes on the line or in the space where it is written, on the staff or on ledger lines. It does not apply to notes that have the same letter name but appear in a higher or lower position on the staff.

1. a) Write the A Major scale ascending and descending. Use accidentals. Use whole notes. Use a center bar line.
   b) Below the scale, label each Tonic (T), Subdominant (SD), Dominant (D) and Leading Tone (LT).

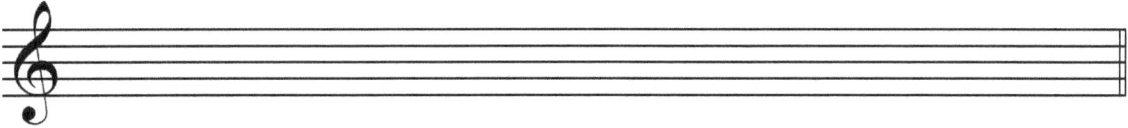

2. a) Write the E♭ Major scale ascending and descending. Use accidentals. Use whole notes. Do not use a center bar line.
   b) Below the scale, label each Tonic (T), Subdominant (SD), Dominant (D) and Leading Tone (LT).

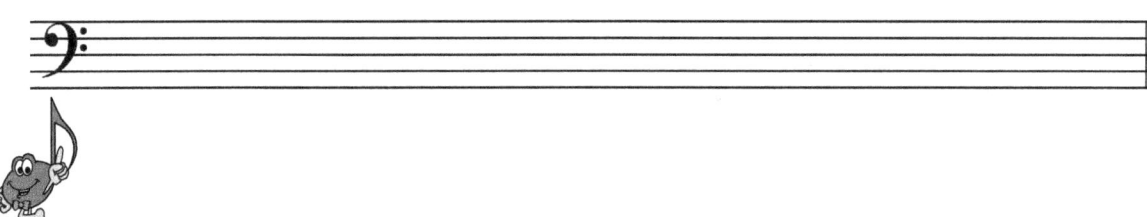

MAJOR SCALES & SCALE DEGREES USING KEY SIGNATURES (Use after Basic Rudiments Page 53)

The **Key Signature** is a group of sharps or flats that indicates the key. Instead of using accidentals, the sharps or flats from the **Major Scale Patterns** are placed in a specific order at the beginning of the staff (directly after the clef sign).

When writing a Major scale using a Key Signature, the notes begin after the Key Signature.

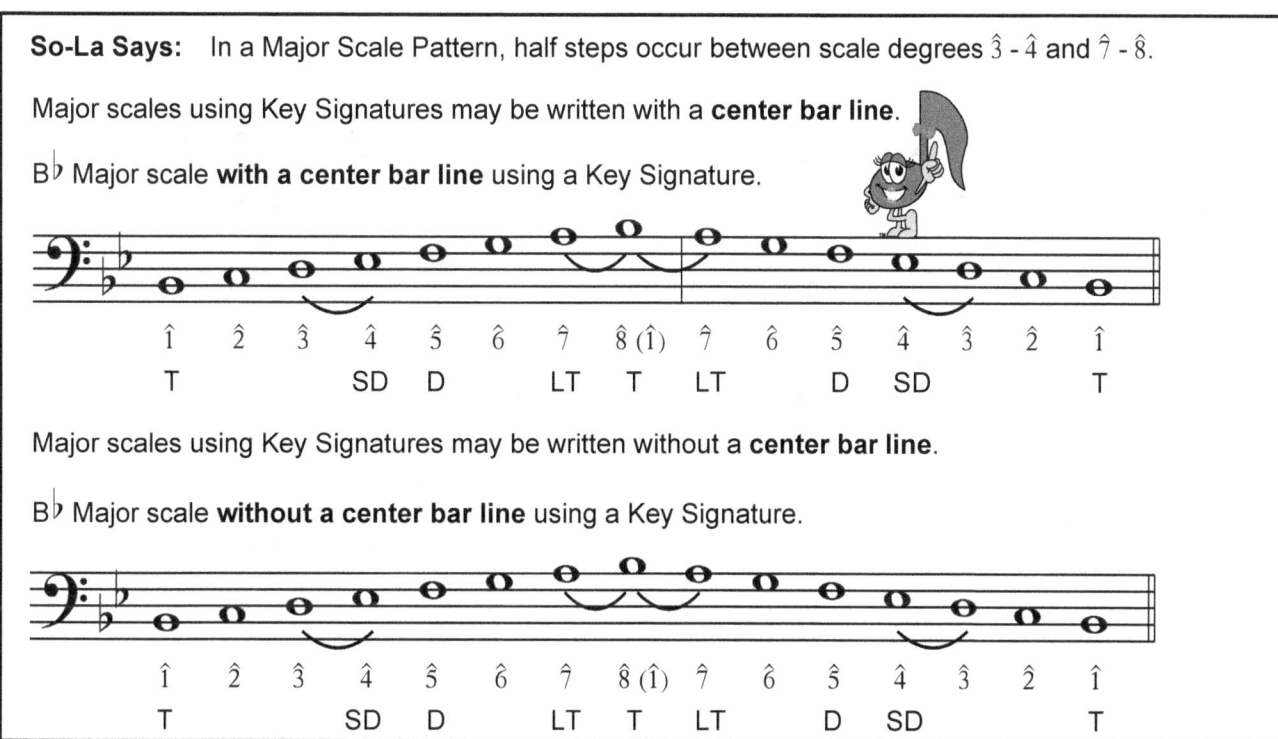

♫ **Ti-Do Tip:** A half step (or semitone) is indicated by a curved line called a "semitone-slur". A semitone-slur is always written below (under) the notes on the staff.

1. a) Write the A Major scale ascending and descending. Use a Key Signature. Use whole notes. Use a center bar line.
   b) Below the scale, number each Scale Degree.
   c) Mark the half steps (semitones) with a semitone-slur.

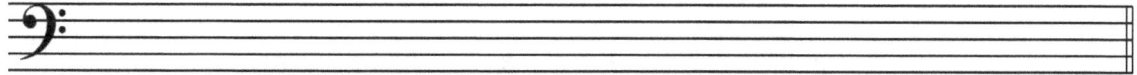

2. a) Write the E♭ Major scale ascending and descending. Use a Key Signature. Use whole notes. Do not use a center bar line.
   b) Below the scale, number each Scale Degree.
   c) Mark the half steps (semitones) with a semitone-slur.

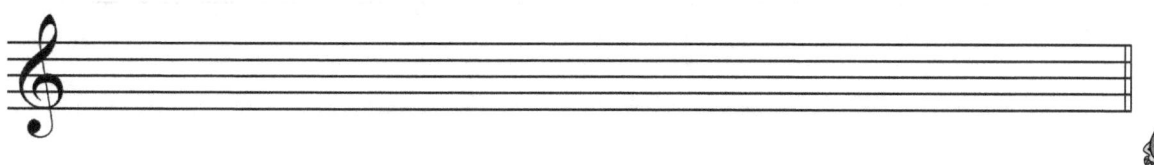

CIRCLE OF FIFTHS - MINOR KEY SIGNATURES (Use after Basic Rudiments Page 72)

Major keys and their relative minor keys share the same Key Signature. The minor key is three half steps (semitones) and three letter names (a minor third) below its relative Major.

♪ **Ti-Do Tip:** From the Major key to its relative minor, go **DOWN** 3 half steps (a minor third).
From the minor key to its relative Major, go **UP** 3 half steps (a minor third).

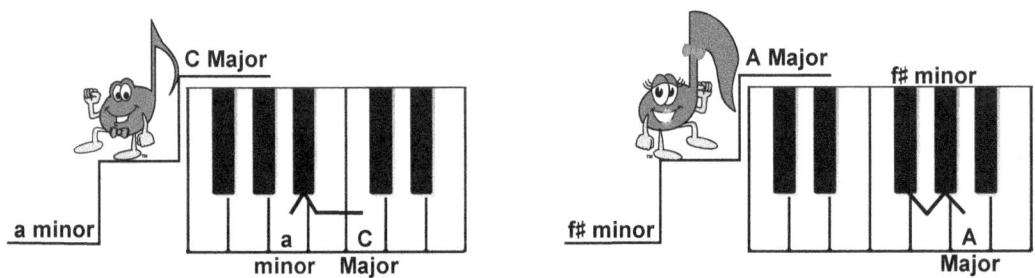

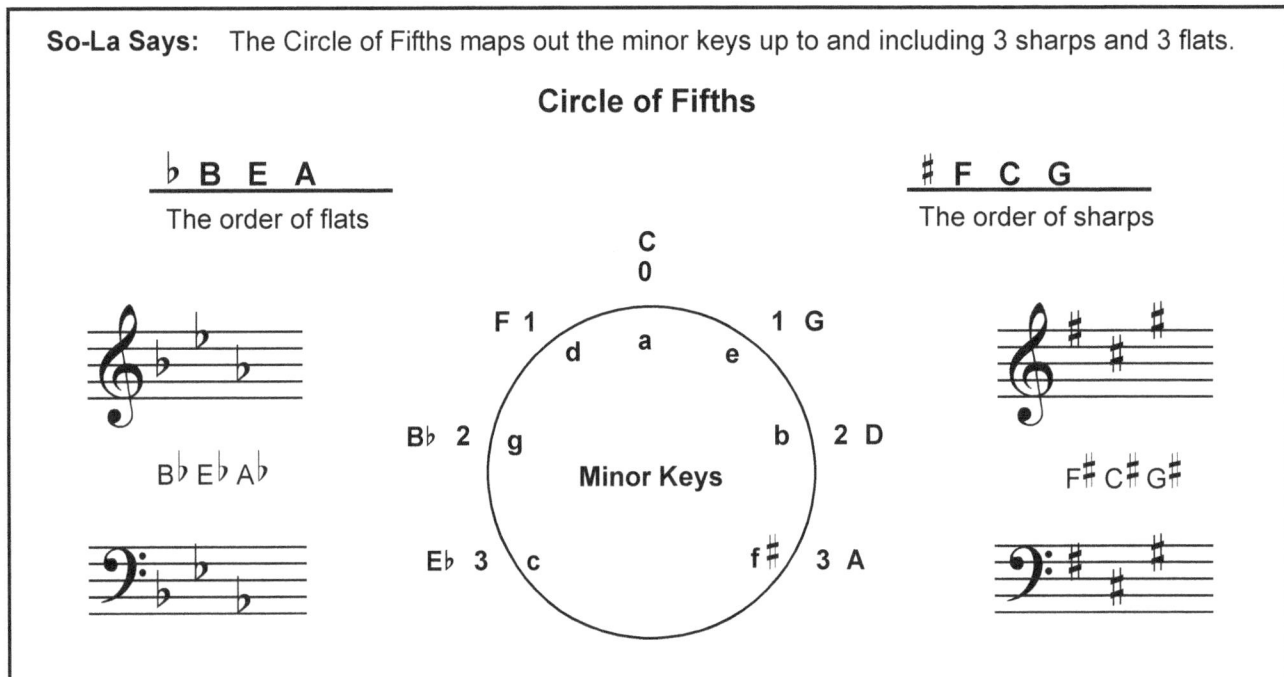

1. Name the Major key and its relative minor key for each of the following Key Signatures.

Major key: _____ _____ _____ _____ _____ _____

minor key: _____ _____ _____ _____ _____ _____

NATURAL MINOR SCALES and SCALE DEGREES (Use after Basic Rudiments Page 75)

A **natural minor scale** is a series of 8 notes in a specific pattern:

$\hat{1}$ whole step $\hat{2}$ half step $\hat{3}$ whole step $\hat{4}$ whole step $\hat{5}$ half step $\hat{6}$ whole step $\hat{7}$ whole step $\hat{8}$ ($\hat{1}$).

A natural minor scale starts on the sixth scale degree of its relative Major scale. A natural minor scale has the same Key Signature as its relative Major scale.

> **So-La Says:** **Scale Degree Names** are technical names given to the specific scale degree numbers.
>
> The **Tonic (T)** $\hat{1}$ is the first note of the scale (establishing the tonality).
> The **Subdominant (SD)** $\hat{4}$ is a 5th below the Upper Tonic (sub = below).
> The **Dominant (D)** $\hat{5}$ is a 5th above the Lower Tonic.
> The **Subtonic (SBT)** $\hat{7}$ is a 2nd (whole step) below the Upper Tonic (a Major 2nd below the Tonic).
>
> e minor natural scale

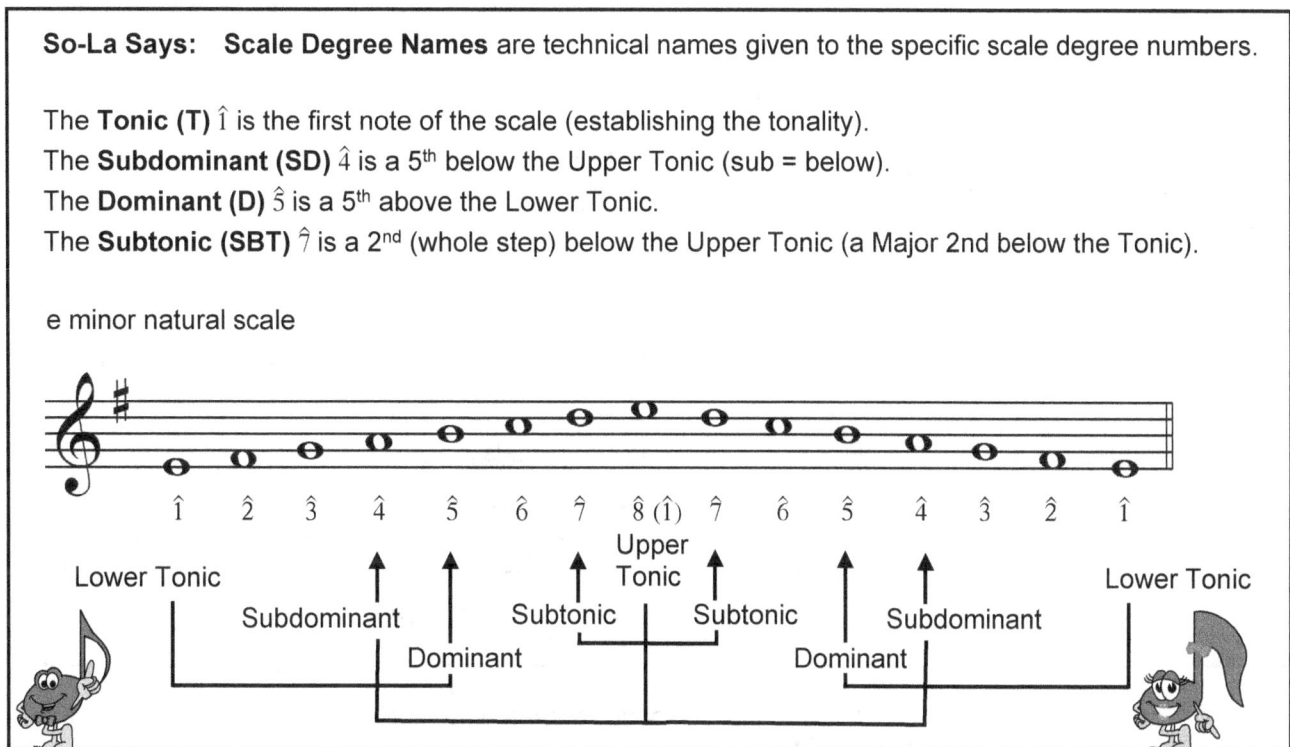

♫ **Ti-Do Tip:** A Leading Tone is a half step below the Tonic. A Subtonic is a whole step below the Tonic.

1. a) Write the Scale Degree Numbers below each note.
   b) Below each scale, label each Tonic (T), Subdominant (SD), Dominant (D) and Subtonic (SBT).

c minor natural scale

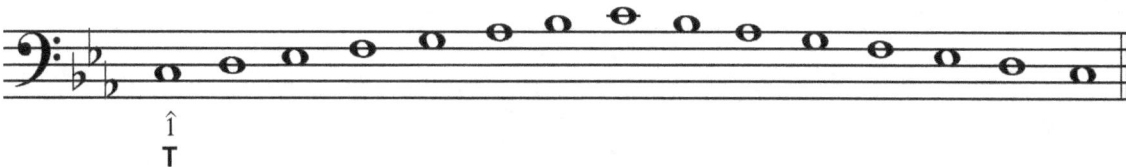

f# minor natural scale

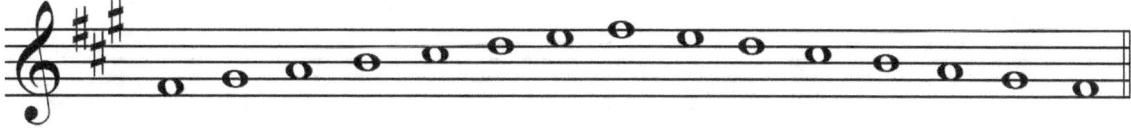

NATURAL MINOR SCALES and SCALE DEGREES USING ACCIDENTALS
(Use after Basic Rudiments Page 75)

A natural minor scale has the same Key Signature as its Relative Major. Nothing else is added.

So-La Says: Natural minor scales using accidentals may be written with or without a **center bar line**.

When writing a natural minor scale using accidentals **with a center bar line**, the accidentals must be repeated in the descending scale because the bar line cancels all the accidentals.

g minor natural scale **with a center bar line** using accidentals.

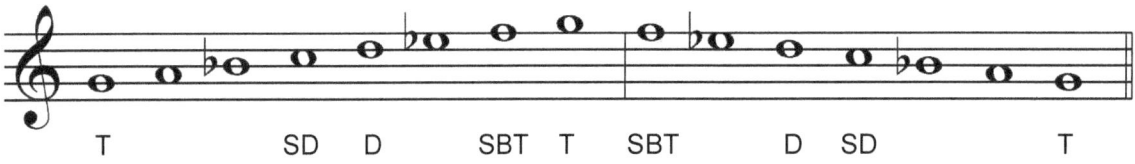

When writing a natural minor scale using accidentals **without a center bar line**, accidentals are written only in the ascending scale.

g minor natural scale **without a center bar line** using accidentals.

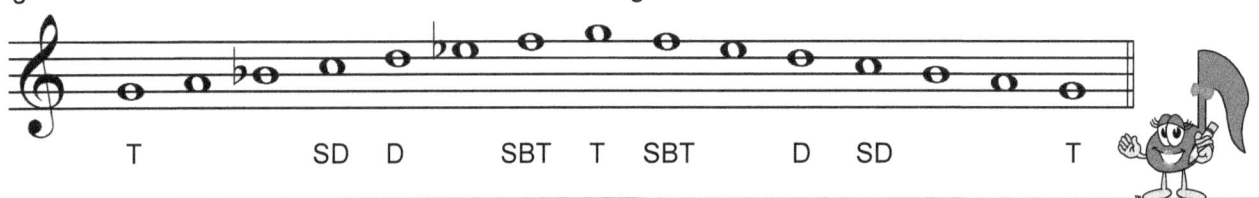

♪ **Ti-Do Tip:** The accidentals used in a natural minor scale are the same sharps or flats found in the Key Signature of its relative Major.

1. a) Write the f# minor natural scale ascending and descending. Use accidentals. Use whole notes. Use a center bar line.
   b) Below the scale, label each Tonic (T), Subdominant (SD), Dominant (D) and Subtonic (SBT).

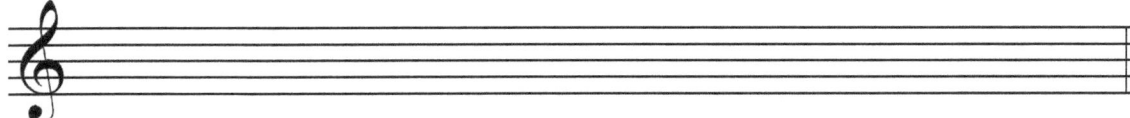

2. a) Write the c minor natural scale ascending and descending. Use accidentals. Use whole notes. Do not use a center bar line.
   b) Below the scale, label each Tonic (T), Subdominant (SD), Dominant (D) and Subtonic (SBT).

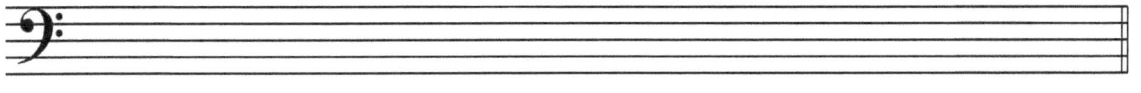

NATURAL MINOR SCALES and SCALE DEGREES USING KEY SIGNATURES
(Use after Basic Rudiments Page 75)

The **Key Signature** is a group of sharps or flats that indicates the key. Instead of using accidentals, the sharps or flats from the **minor Scale Patterns** are placed in a specific order at the beginning of the staff (directly after the clef sign).

In the natural minor scale, nothing else is added. This means that there are no extra accidentals.

So-La Says: A natural minor scale pattern has half steps between scale degrees $\hat{2}$ - $\hat{3}$ and $\hat{5}$ - $\hat{6}$.

Natural minor scales using Key Signatures may be written with a **center bar line**.

g minor natural scale **with a center bar line** using a Key Signature.

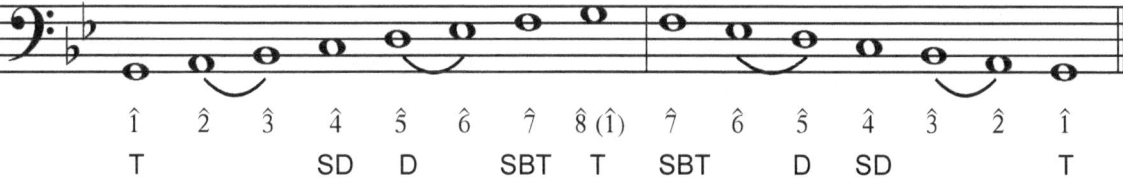

Natural minor scales using Key Signatures may be written without a **center bar line**.

g minor natural scale **without a center bar line** using a Key Signature.

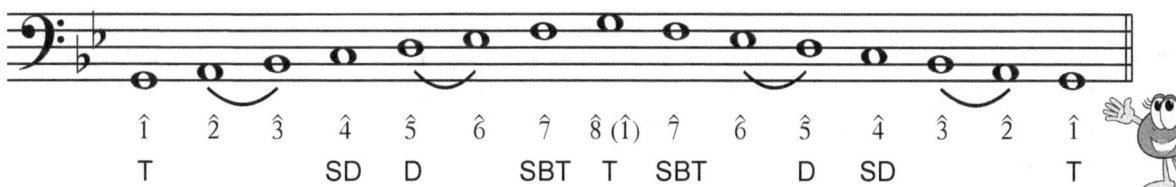

♪ **Ti-Do Tip:** A half step (or semitone) is indicated by a curved line called a "semitone-slur". A semitone-slur is always written below (under) the notes on the staff.

1. a) Write the f♯ minor natural scale ascending and descending. Use a Key Signature. Use whole notes. Use a center bar line.
   b) Below the scale, number each Scale Degree.
   c) Mark the half steps (semitones) with a semitone-slur.

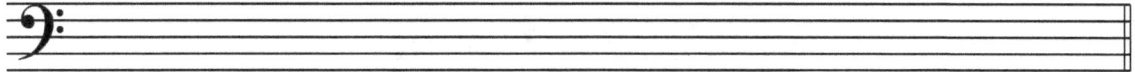

2. a) Write the c minor natural scale ascending and descending. Use a Key Signature. Use whole notes. Do not use a center bar line.
   b) Below the scale, number each Scale Degree.
   c) Mark the half steps (semitones) with a semitone-slur.

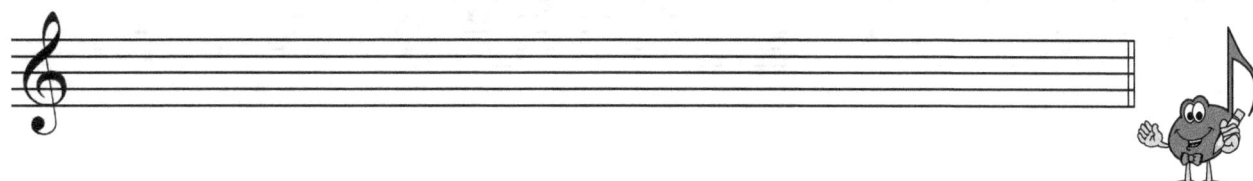

HARMONIC MINOR SCALES and SCALE DEGREES (Use after Basic Rudiments Page 77)

A **harmonic minor scale** is a series of 8 notes in a specific pattern:

$\hat{1}$ whole step $\hat{2}$ half step $\hat{3}$ whole step $\hat{4}$ whole step $\hat{5}$ half step $\hat{6}$ whole + half step $\hat{7}$ half step $\hat{8}$ ($\hat{1}$).

A **harmonic minor scale** has the same Key Signature as its relative Major. In the harmonic minor scale, the 7th note is raised one chromatic half step (semitone) ascending and descending.

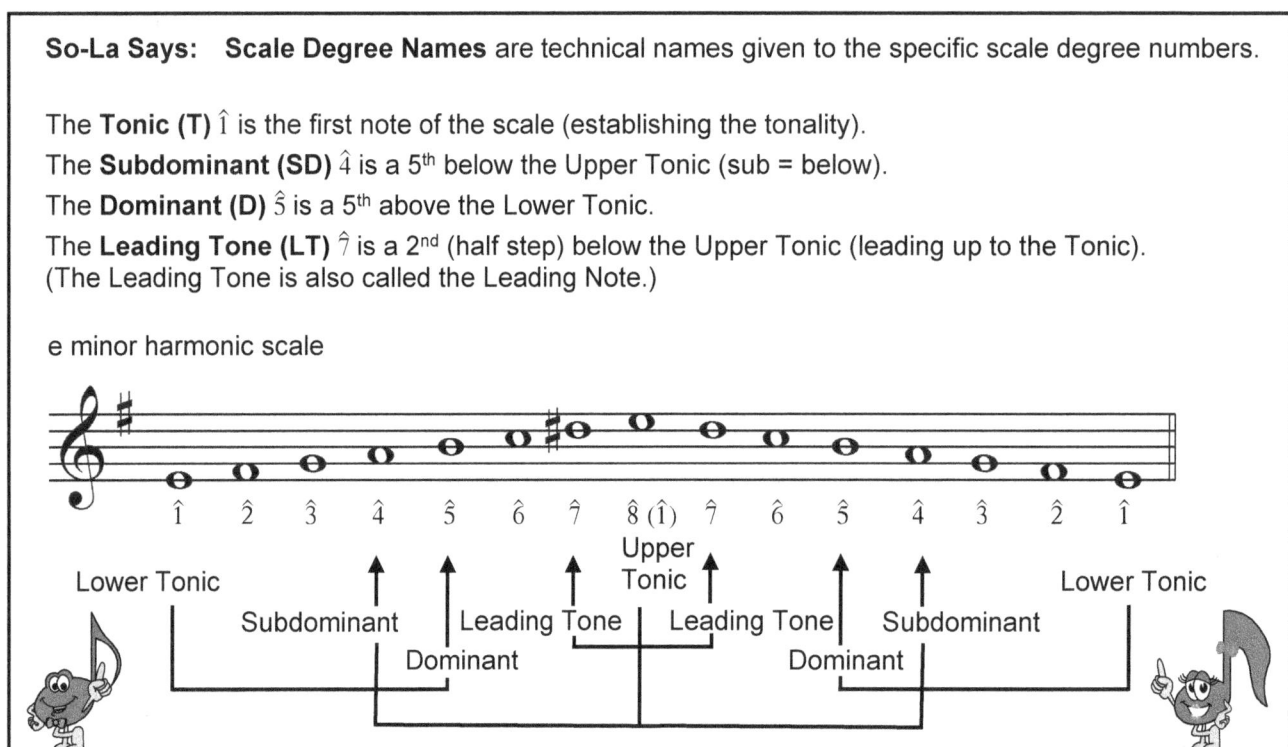

So-La Says: Scale Degree Names are technical names given to the specific scale degree numbers.

The **Tonic (T)** $\hat{1}$ is the first note of the scale (establishing the tonality).
The **Subdominant (SD)** $\hat{4}$ is a 5th below the Upper Tonic (sub = below).
The **Dominant (D)** $\hat{5}$ is a 5th above the Lower Tonic.
The **Leading Tone (LT)** $\hat{7}$ is a 2nd (half step) below the Upper Tonic (leading up to the Tonic).
(The Leading Tone is also called the Leading Note.)

♪ **Ti-Do Tip:** An accidental is used to raise the 7th note a chromatic half step ascending and descending.

1. a) Write the Scale Degree Numbers below each note.
   b) Below each scale, label each Tonic (T), Subdominant (SD), Dominant (D) and Leading Tone (LT).

c minor harmonic scale

$\hat{1}$
T

f♯ minor harmonic scale

HARMONIC MINOR SCALES and SCALE DEGREES USING ACCIDENTALS
(Use after Basic Rudiments Page 77)

A **harmonic minor scale** has the same Key Signature as its relative Major. In the harmonic minor scale, the 7th note is raised one chromatic half step (semitone) ascending and descending.

So-La Says: Harmonic minor scales using accidentals may be written with or without a **center bar line**.

When writing a harmonic minor scale using accidentals **with a center bar line**, the accidentals must be repeated in the descending scale because the bar line cancels all the accidentals.

g minor harmonic scale **with a center bar line** using accidentals.

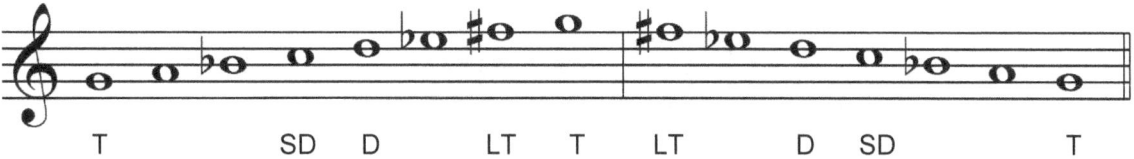

T   SD   D   LT   T   LT   D   SD   T

When writing a harmonic minor scale using accidentals **without a center bar line**, accidentals are written only in the ascending scale.

g minor harmonic scale **without a center bar line** using accidentals.

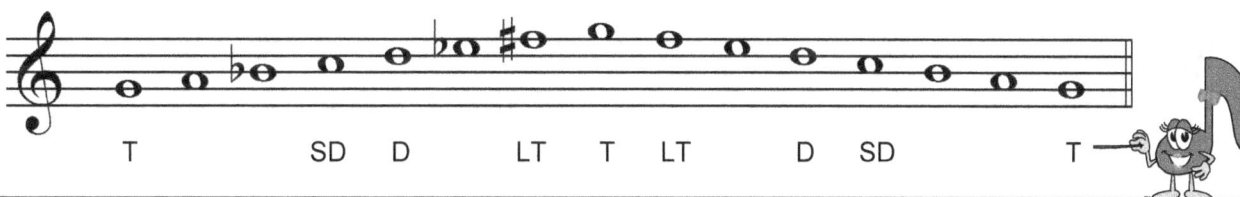

T   SD   D   LT   T   LT   D   SD   T

♪ **Ti-Do Tip:** The accidentals used in a harmonic minor scale are the same sharps or flats found in the Key Signature of its relative Major, with the addition of the accidental for the raised 7th.

1. a) Write the f# sharp minor harmonic scale ascending and descending. Use accidentals. Use whole notes. Use a center bar line.
   b) Below the scale, label each Tonic (T), Subdominant (SD), Dominant (D) and Leading Tone (LT).

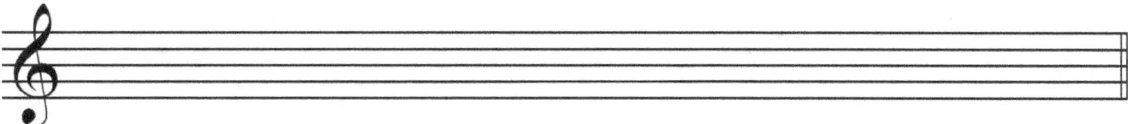

2. a) Write the c minor harmonic scale ascending and descending. Use accidentals. Use whole notes. Do not use a center bar line.
   b) Below the scale, label each Tonic (T), Subdominant (SD), Dominant (D) and Leading Tone (LT).

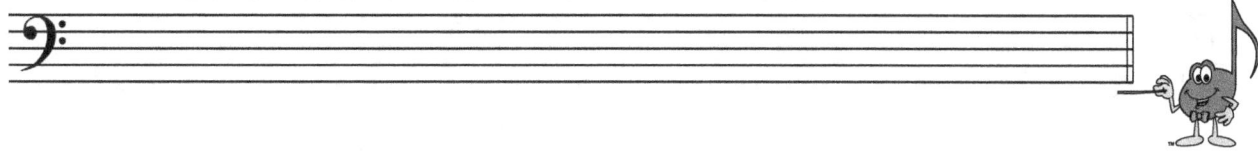

HARMONIC MINOR SCALES and SCALE DEGREES USING KEY SIGNATURES
(Use after Basic Rudiments Page 77)

The **Key Signature** is a group of sharps or flats that indicates the key. The accidental used to raise the Leading Tone in the harmonic minor scale is not written as part of the Key Signature.

In the harmonic minor scale, the raised 7th note is always written as an accidental.

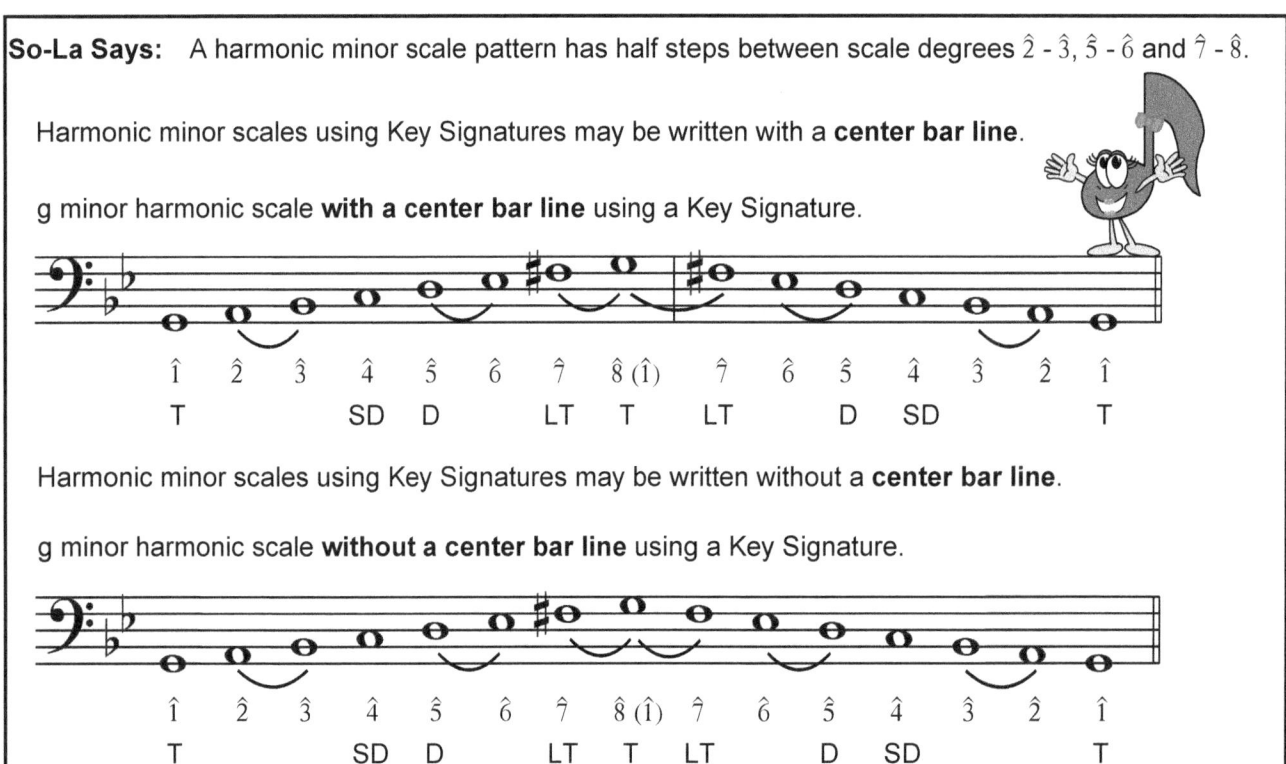

♫ **Ti-Do Tip:** In a harmonic minor scale, the distance between the $\hat{6}$ - $\hat{7}$ notes is a Whole Step plus a Half Step (3 half steps).

1. a) Write the f# minor harmonic scale ascending and descending. Use a Key Signature and any necessary accidentals. Use whole notes. Use a center bar line.
   b) Below the scale, number each Scale Degree.
   c) Mark the half steps (semitones) with a semitone-slur.

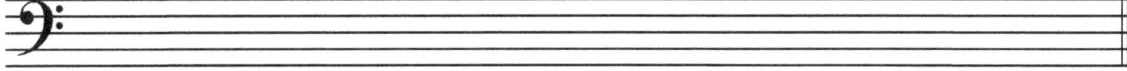

2. a) Write the c minor harmonic scale ascending and descending. Use a Key Signature and any necessary accidentals. Use whole notes. Do not use a center bar line.
   b) Below the scale, number each Scale Degree.
   c) Mark the half steps (semitones) with a semitone-slur.

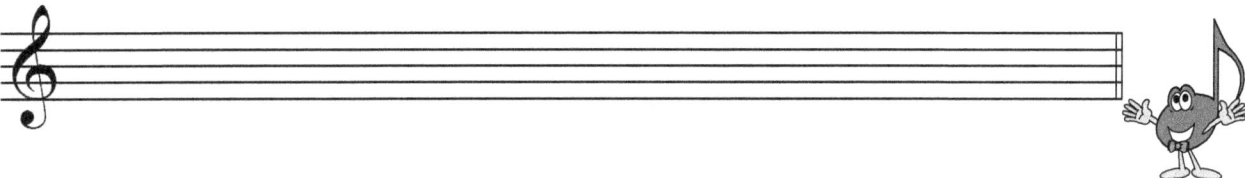

MELODIC MINOR SCALES and SCALE DEGREES (Use after Basic Rudiments Page 79)

A **melodic minor scale** is a series of 8 notes in a specific pattern:

Ascending: $\hat{1}$ whole step $\hat{2}$ half step $\hat{3}$ whole step $\hat{4}$ whole step $\hat{5}$ whole step (raised) $\hat{6}$ whole step (raised) $\hat{7}$ half step $\hat{8}$ ($\hat{1}$).

Descending: $\hat{8}$ ($\hat{1}$) whole step (lowered) $\hat{7}$ whole step (lowered) $\hat{6}$ half step $\hat{5}$ whole step $\hat{4}$ whole step $\hat{3}$ half step $\hat{2}$ whole step $\hat{1}$.

> **So-La Says:** **Scale Degree Names** are technical names given to the specific scale degree numbers.
>
> The **Tonic (T)** $\hat{1}$ is the first note of the scale (establishing the tonality).
> The **Subdominant (SD)** $\hat{4}$ is a 5th below the Upper Tonic (sub = below).
> The **Dominant (D)** $\hat{5}$ is a 5th above the Lower Tonic.
> The **ascending Leading Tone (LT)** $\hat{7}$ is a 2nd (half step) below the Upper Tonic.
> The **descending Subtonic (SBT)** $\hat{7}$ is a 2nd (whole step) below the Upper Tonic.
>
> e minor melodic scale
>
>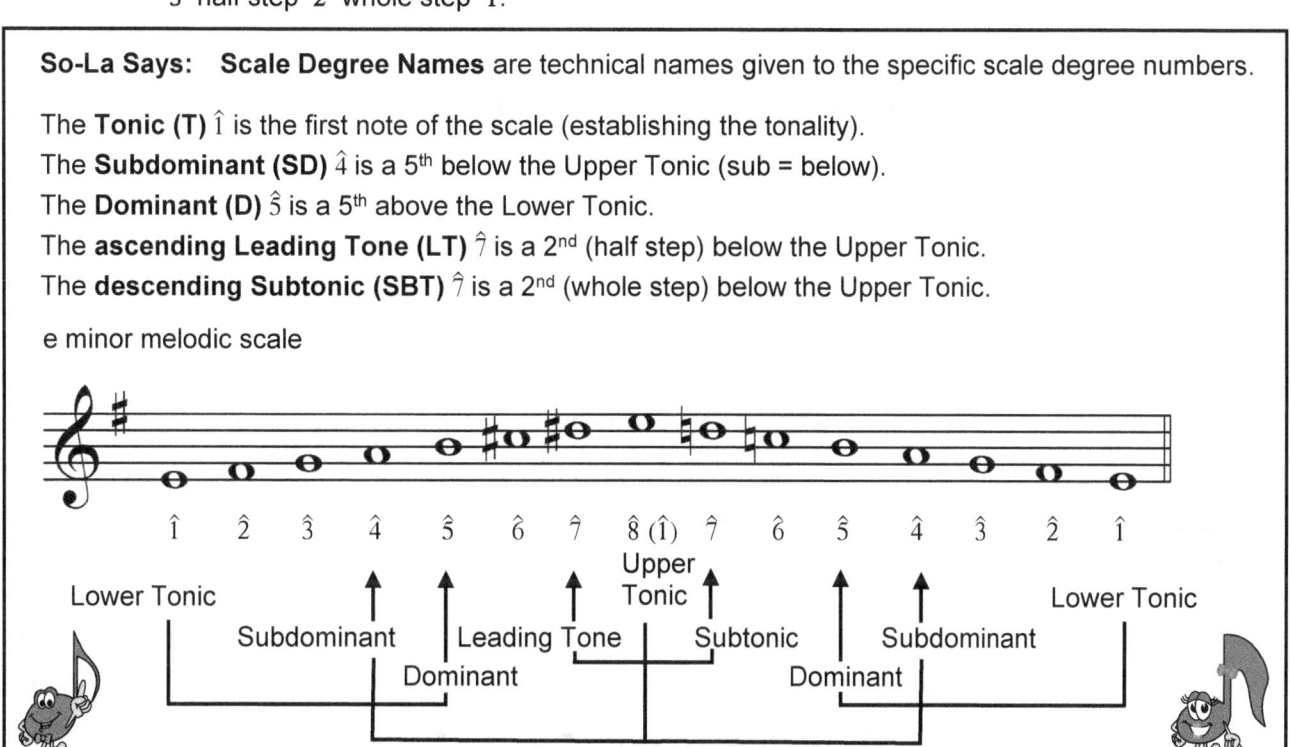

♫ **Ti-Do Tip:** The descending melodic minor scale is the same as the natural minor scale.

1. a) Write the Scale Degree Numbers below each note.
   b) Below each scale, label each Tonic (T), Subdominant (SD), Dominant (D), Leading Tone (LT) and Subtonic (SBT).

c minor melodic scale

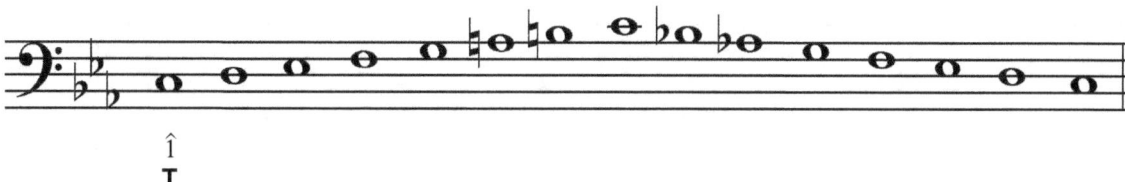

$\hat{1}$
T

f# minor melodic scale

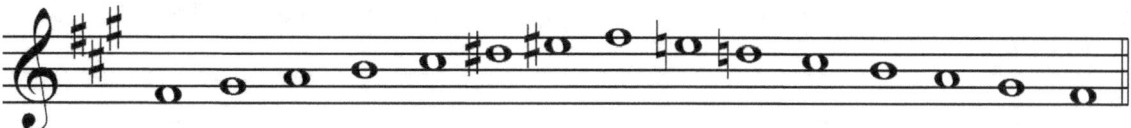

MELODIC MINOR SCALES and SCALE DEGREES USING ACCIDENTALS
(Use after Basic Rudiments Page 79)

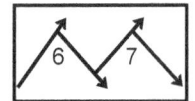

A **melodic minor scale** has the same Key Signature as its relative Major. In the melodic minor scale, the 6th and 7th notes are raised one chromatic half step (semitone) ascending and lowered one chromatic half step (semitone) descending.

So-La Says: Melodic minor scales using accidentals may be written with or without a **center bar line**.

When writing a melodic minor scale using accidentals **with a center bar line**, the accidentals must be rewritten in the descending scale because the bar line cancels all the accidentals.

g minor melodic scale **with a center bar line** using accidentals.

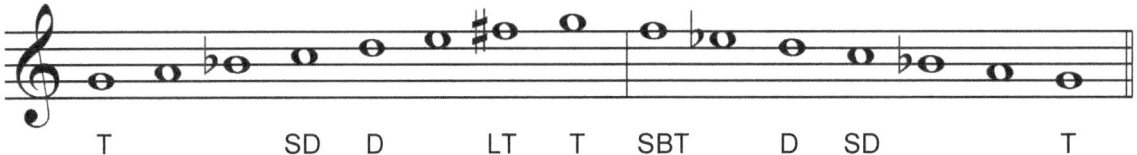

When writing a melodic minor scale using accidentals **without a center bar line**, accidentals are required in the descending scale to lower the 7th and 6th notes.

g minor melodic scale **without a center bar line** using accidentals.

♩ **Ti-Do Tip:** When using accidentals, a natural sign is not required to raise a flat in the ascending scale. A natural sign is used only when there is a previous accidental to cancel.

1. a) Write the f# minor melodic scale ascending and descending. Use accidentals. Use whole notes. Use a center bar line.
   b) Below the scale, label each Tonic (T), Subdominant (SD), Dominant (D), Leading Tone (LT) and Subtonic (SBT).

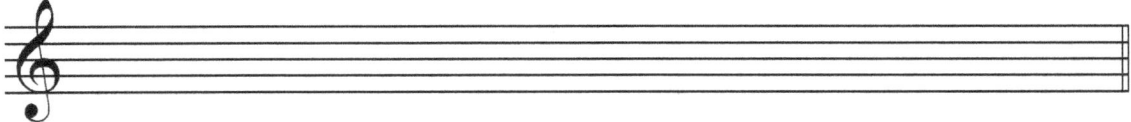

2. a) Write the c minor melodic scale ascending and descending. Use accidentals. Use whole notes. Do not use a center bar line.
   b) Below the scale, label each Tonic (T), Subdominant (SD), Dominant (D), Leading Tone (LT) and Subtonic (SBT).

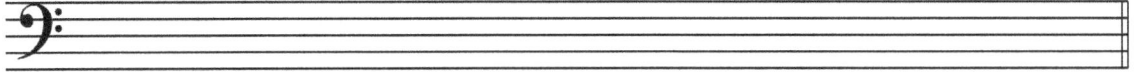

MELODIC MINOR SCALES and SCALE DEGREES USING KEY SIGNATURES
(Use after Basic Rudiments Page 79)

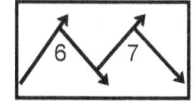

The **Key Signature** is a group of sharps or flats that indicates the key. The accidentals used to raise the ascending 6th and 7th notes and to lower the descending 7th and 6th notes are not written as part of the Key Signature. They are always written as accidentals.

So-La Says: The ascending melodic minor Scale Pattern has half steps between scale degrees $\hat{2}$ - $\hat{3}$ and $\hat{7}$ - $\hat{8}$. The descending melodic minor has half steps between the $\hat{6}$ - $\hat{5}$ and $\hat{3}$ - $\hat{2}$.

Melodic minor scales using Key Signatures may be written with a **center bar line**.

g minor melodic scale **with a center bar line** using a Key Signature.

Melodic minor scales using Key Signatures may be written without a **center bar line**.

g minor melodic scale **without a center bar line** using a Key Signature.

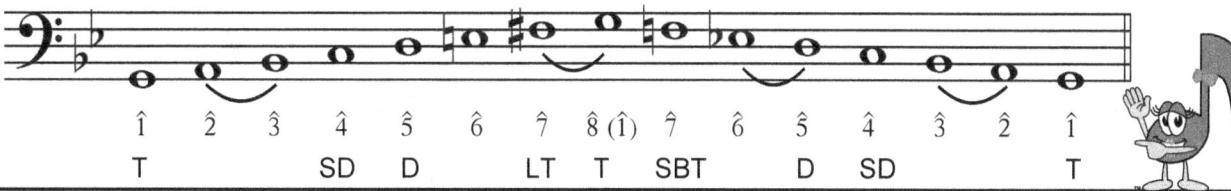

♫ **Ti-Do Tip:** In a melodic minor scale, the descending scale is the same as the natural minor scale.

1. a) Write the f# minor melodic scale ascending and descending. Use a Key Signature and any necessary accidentals. Use whole notes. Use a center bar line.
   b) Below the scale, number each Scale Degree.
   c) Mark the half steps (semitones) with a semitone-slur.

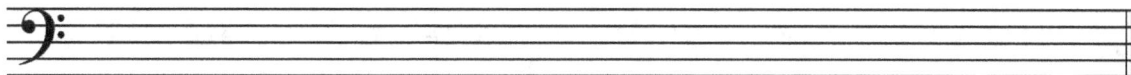

2. a) Write the c minor melodic scale ascending and descending. Use a Key Signature and any necessary accidentals. Use whole notes. Do not use a center bar line.
   b) Below the scale, number each Scale Degree.
   c) Mark the half steps (semitones) with a semitone-slur.

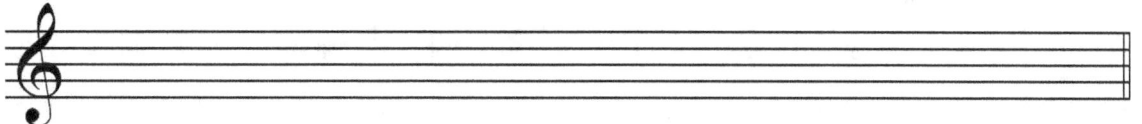

SAME WORD - DIFFERENT CONCEPT (Use after Basic Rudiments Page 80)

In music, the same words can be used to describe different concepts. Words such as harmonic, melodic, chromatic and diatonic have different meanings when they refer to different concepts.

Harmony is the sound that results when two or more tones are played or sung at the same time.

Melody is a series of tones of different pitches arranged in a rhythmic pattern.

So-La Says: Harmonic intervals and harmonic minor scales both use the word "Harmonic" (harmony).

Melodic intervals and melodic minor scales both use the word "Melodic" (melody).

A **Harmonic** interval is written one note **above** the other, both played at the same time (together).

A **Melodic** interval is written one note **beside** the other, played one note after the other (separately).

Harmonic minor scale - Raise the 7th note (one half step) ascending and descending.

Melodic minor scale - Raise the 6th and 7th notes (one half step) ascending and lower the 7th and 6th notes (one half step) descending.

---

1. Check (✓) the correct answer.

   a) An interval written one note beside the other, separately.   ☐ Harmonic   or   ☐ Melodic

   b) An interval written one note above the other, together.   ☐ Harmonic   or   ☐ Melodic

   c) A minor scale with a raised 7th ascending and descending.   ☐ Harmonic   or   ☐ Melodic

Chromatic is a term that refers to a tone that is not in the key of the composition. It is Greek for "color".

Diatonic is a term that means staying (for the most part) within a key or scale.

So-La Says: Chromatic half steps and chromatic scales both use notes not found in the key or scale.

Diatonic half steps and diatonic scales both use notes found in the key or scale.

A **Chromatic** half step (semitone) is written using the same letter names.

A **Diatonic** half step (semitone) is written using different (neighboring) letter names.

A **Chromatic** scale is one that goes up or down in a series of half steps.

A **Diatonic** scale is one that has a recognized key (Major or minor).

---

2. Check (✓) the correct answer.

   a) A half step using different letter names.   ☐ Chromatic   or   ☐ Diatonic

   b) A half step using the same letter names.   ☐ Chromatic   or   ☐ Diatonic

   c) A scale that has a recognized key (Major or minor).   ☐ Chromatic   or   ☐ Diatonic

INTERVAL REVIEW (Use after Basic Rudiments Page 80)

An **Interval** is the distance in pitch between two notes - a lower note and a higher note. An interval can be written using accidentals or a Key Signature. The lower note determines the Major Key Signature.

> **So-La Says:** An interval is always based on the notes of the Major scale. Use the Major Key Signature of the lower note to help write or identify intervals.
>
> **Perfect Intervals** are 1, 4, 5 and 8. The abbreviation for Perfect is "Per".
>
> **Major Intervals** are 2, 3, 6 and 7. The abbreviation for Major is "Maj".
>
> A **minor interval** is one chromatic half step smaller than a Major interval. Only the intervals 2, 3, 6 and 7 can become minor. The abbreviation for minor is "min".

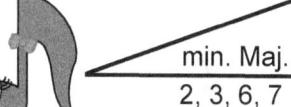

♩ **Ti-Do Tip:** The **size** of the interval is the interval number.
The **quality** of the interval is whether it is Major, minor or Perfect.

1. Write the following harmonic intervals above each given note. Use whole notes. Use accidentals when necessary.

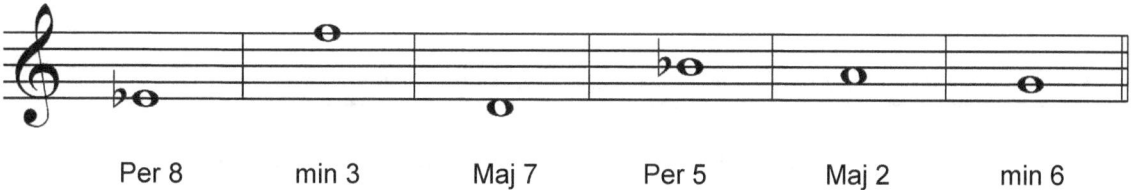

Per 8   min 3   Maj 7   Per 5   Maj 2   min 6

2. Observing the Major Key Signatures, write the following melodic intervals above each given note. Use whole notes. Use accidentals when necessary.

Maj 3   Per 1   min 2   Maj 6   Per 4   min 7

3. Name the following intervals.

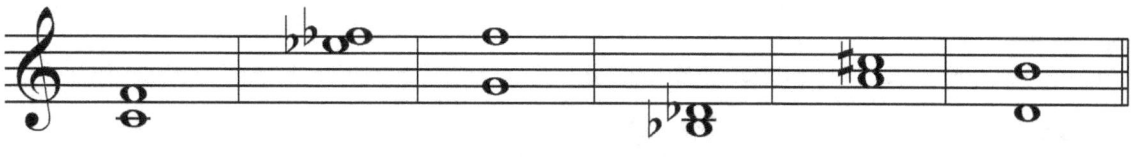

___ ___ ___ ___ ___ ___

>
> ♩ **Ti-Do Time:** LISTEN as your Teacher plays the intervals on Page 25.
> Identify if the interval played is a harmonic interval or a melodic interval.
> Identify the name (size and quality) of each interval.

FUNCTIONAL CHORD SYMBOLS - TONIC TRIADS in MAJOR and MINOR KEYS
(Use after Basic Rudiments Page 86)

The triad built on Scale Degree 1̂ of the Major scale is called the **Tonic** Triad. It is a Major triad. The **Functional Chord Symbol** for the Major Tonic Triad is I.

The triad built on Scale Degree 1̂ of the harmonic minor scale is called the **Tonic** Triad. It is a minor triad. The **Functional Chord Symbol** for the minor Tonic Triad is i.

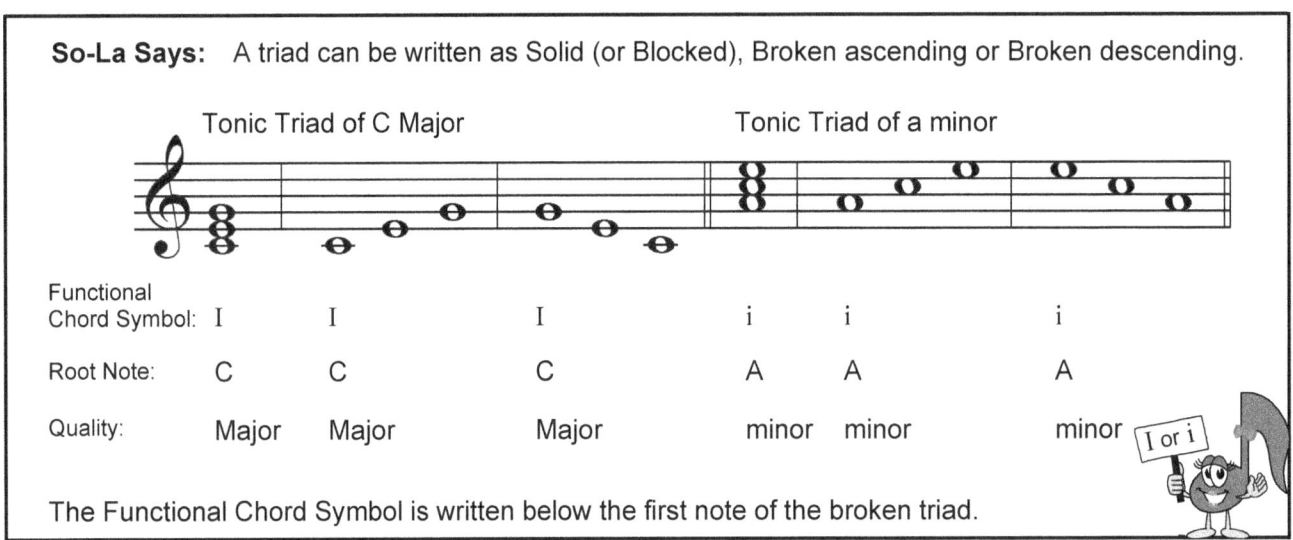

♪ **Ti-Do Tip:** A Major triad uses an upper case Roman Numeral. A minor triad uses a lower case.

1. a) Name the Major key.
   b) Identify the Functional Chord Symbol for each triad.

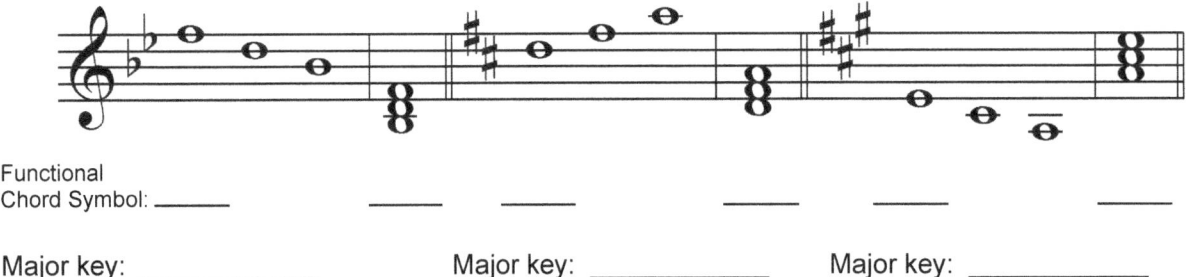

Functional
Chord Symbol: _____   _____   _____   _____   _____

Major key: _____   Major key: _____   Major key: _____

2. a) Name the minor key.
   b) Identify the Functional Chord Symbol for each triad.

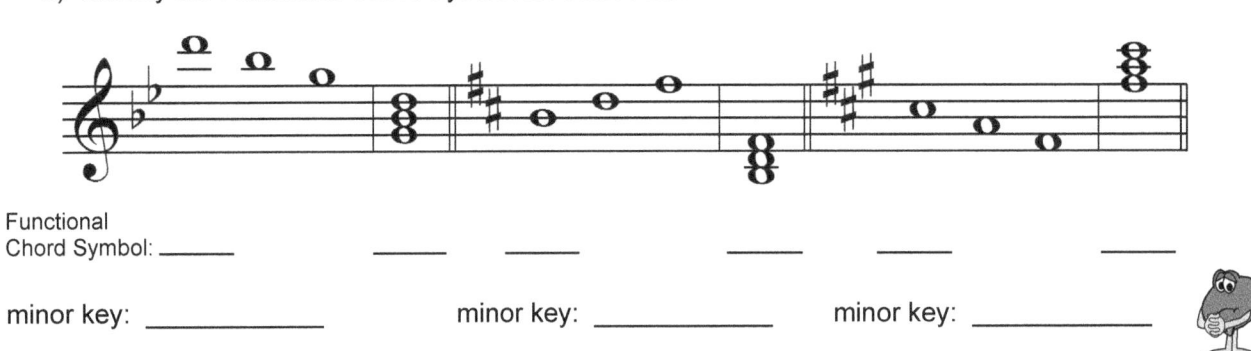

Functional
Chord Symbol: _____   _____   _____   _____   _____

minor key: _____   minor key: _____   minor key: _____

ROOT/QUALITY CHORD SYMBOLS - TONIC TRIADS in MAJOR and MINOR KEYS
(Use after Basic Rudiments Page 86)

Root/Quality Chord Symbols are Letter Names that indicate the quality (Major or minor) of a triad.

An upper case letter indicates a Major triad. (Example: D = D Major triad)
An upper case letter with an "m" after it indicates a minor triad. (Example: Dm = d minor triad)

So-La Says: The Root/Quality Chord Symbol is written above the first note of the triad.
The Functional Chord Symbol is written below the first note of the triad.

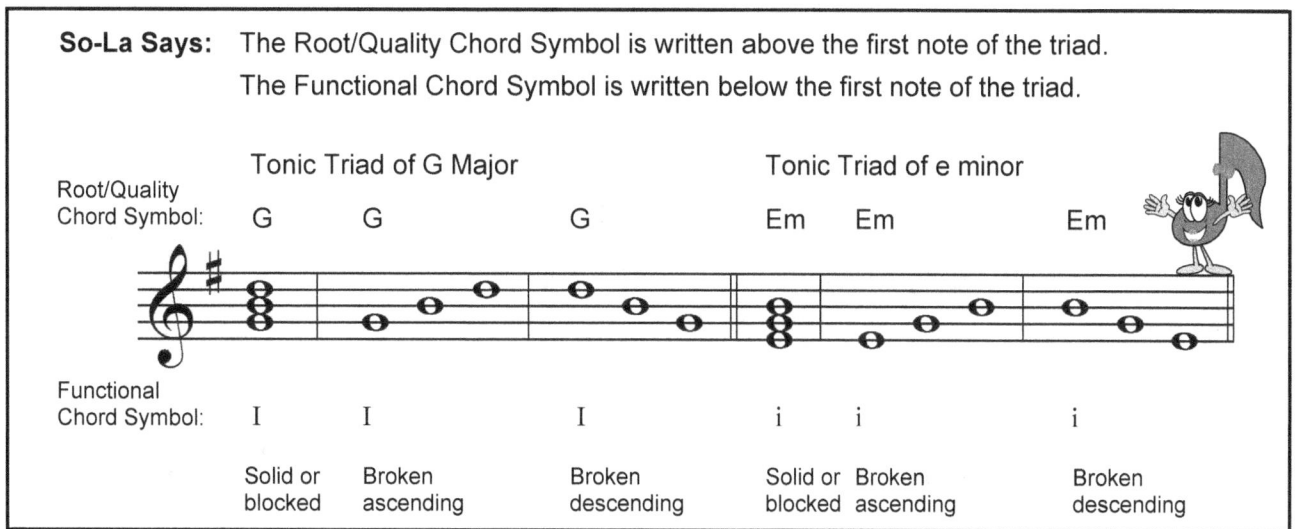

♪ **Ti-Do Tip:** The Tonic Triad of a Major key is a Major triad.
The Tonic Triad of a minor key is a minor triad.

1. a) Name the Root/Quality Chord Symbol above each triad.
   b) Identify the Functional Chord Symbol below each triad.

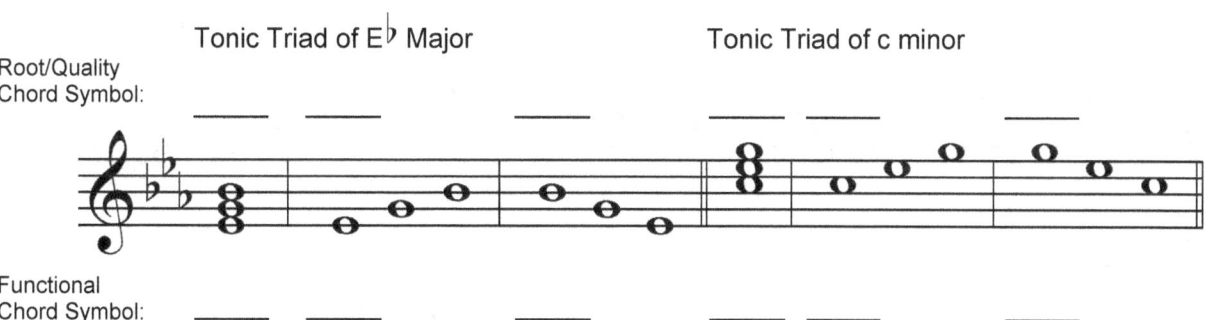

2. Write the following triads. Use whole notes.

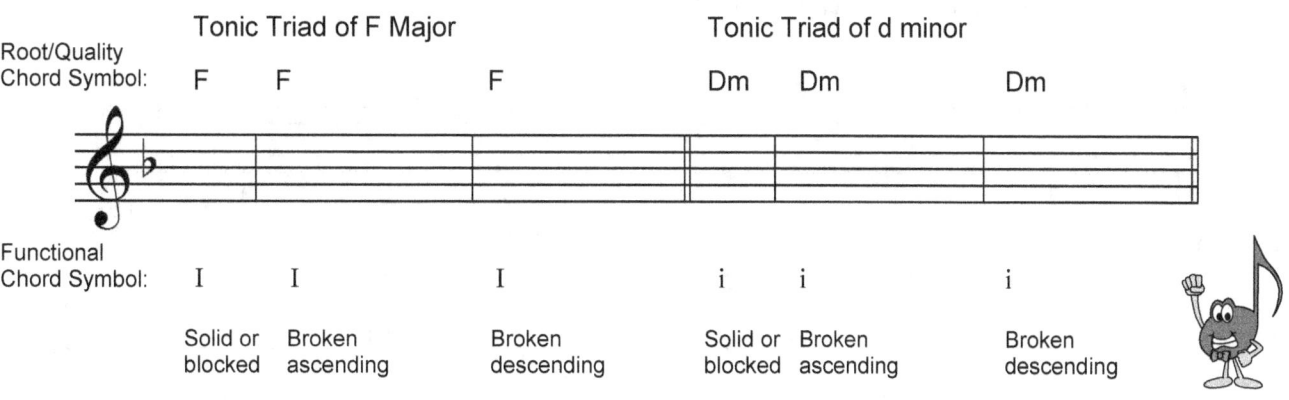

UltimateMusicTheory.com © Copyright 2017 Gloryland Publishing. All Rights Reserved.

FUNCTIONAL CHORD SYMBOLS - SUBDOMINANT TRIADS in MAJOR and MINOR KEYS
(Use after Basic Rudiments Page 87)

The triad built on Scale Degree $\hat{4}$ of the Major scale is called the **Subdominant** Triad. It is a Major triad. The **Functional Chord Symbol** for the Major Subdominant Triad is IV.

The triad built on Scale Degree $\hat{4}$ of the harmonic minor scale is called the **Subdominant** Triad. It is a minor triad. The **Functional Chord Symbol** for the minor Subdominant Triad is iv.

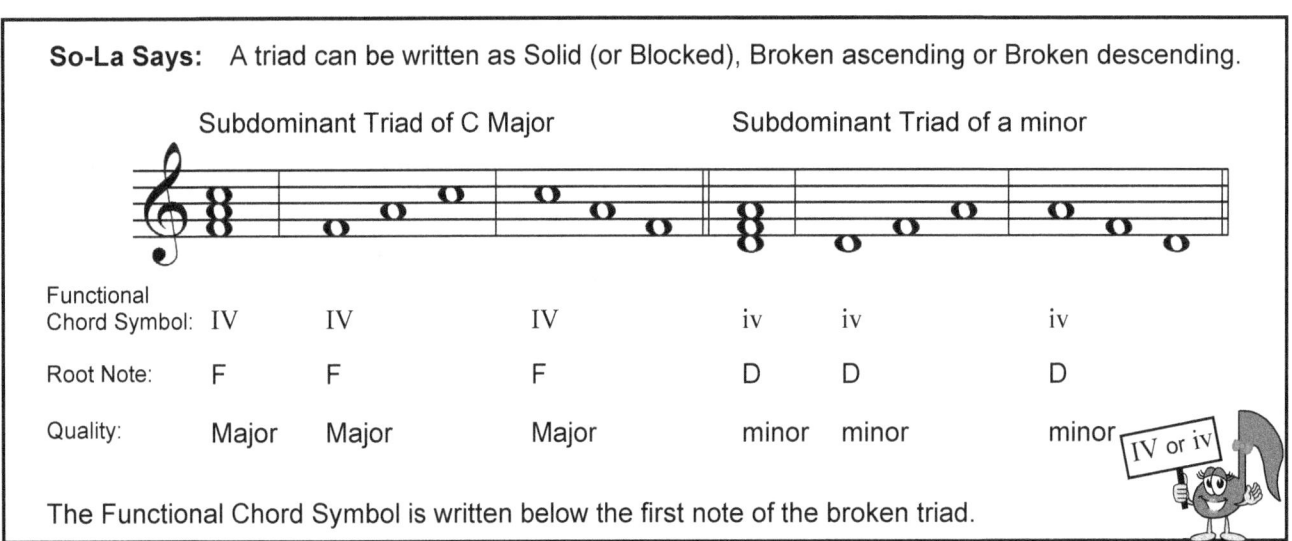

♫ **Ti-Do Tip:** A Major triad uses an upper case Roman Numeral. A minor triad uses a lower case.

1. a) Name the Major key.
   b) Identify the Functional Chord Symbol for each triad.

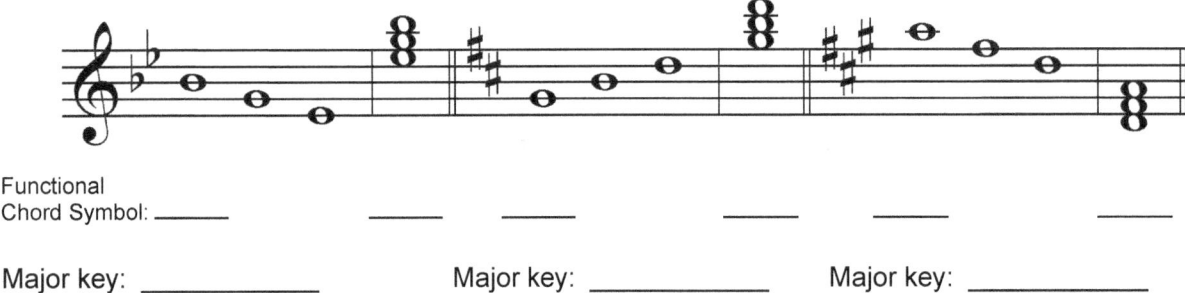

Functional
Chord Symbol: _____   _____   _____   _____   _____   _____

Major key: _____   Major key: _____   Major key: _____

2. a) Name the minor key.
   b) Identify the Functional Chord Symbol for each triad.

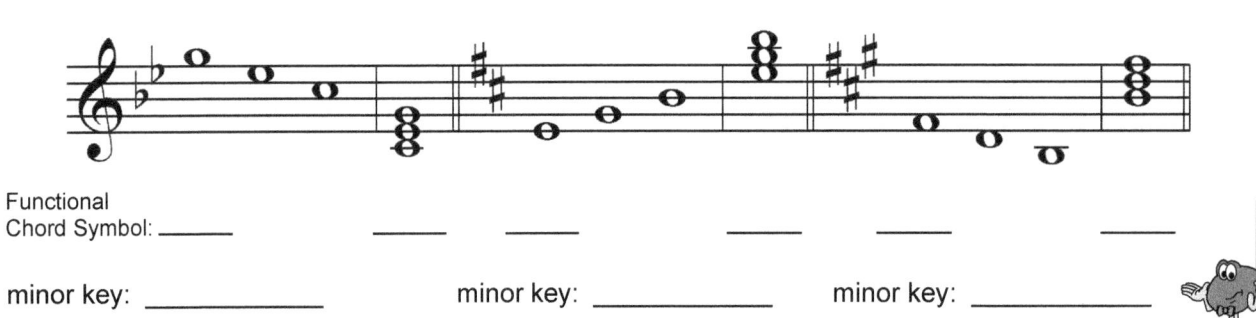

Functional
Chord Symbol: _____   _____   _____   _____   _____   _____

minor key: _____   minor key: _____   minor key: _____

ROOT/QUALITY CHORD SYMBOLS - SUBDOMINANT TRIADS in MAJOR and MINOR KEYS
(Use after Basic Rudiments Page 87)

Root/Quality Chord Symbols are Letter Names that indicate the quality (Major or minor) of a triad.

An upper case letter indicates a Major triad. (Example: D = D Major triad)
An upper case letter with an "m" after it indicates a minor triad. (Example: Dm = d minor triad)

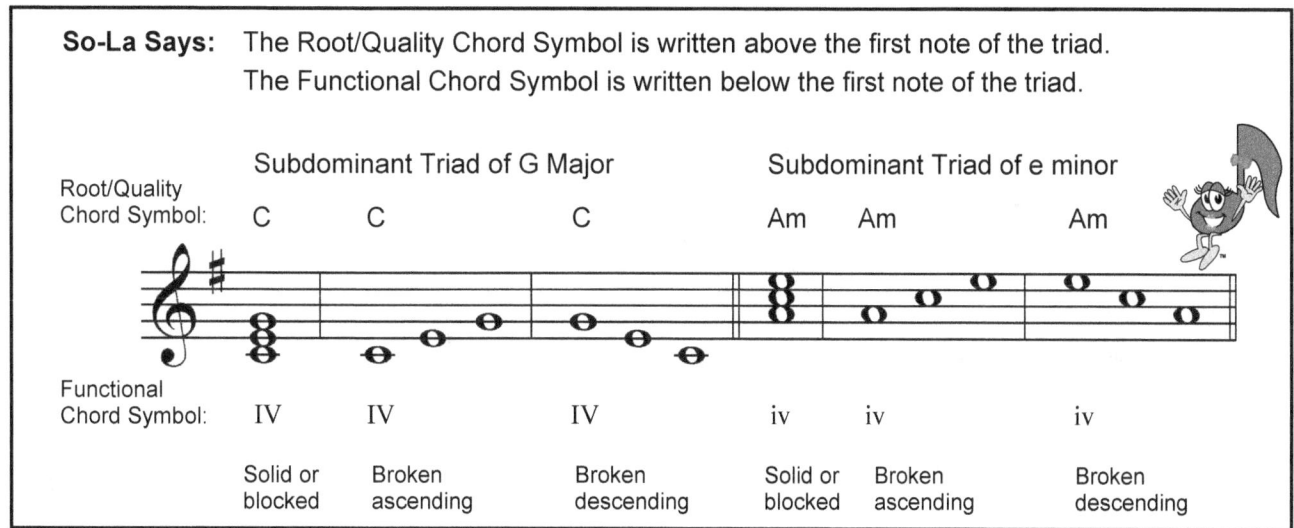

♫ **Ti-Do Tip:** The Subdominant Triad of a Major key is a Major triad.
The Subdominant Triad of a minor key is a minor triad.

1. a) Name the Root/Quality Chord Symbol above each triad.
   b) Identify the Functional Chord Symbol below each triad.

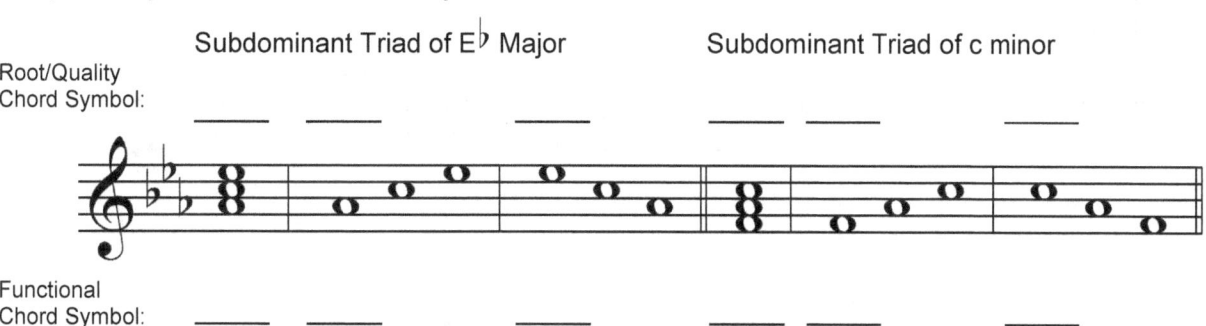

2. Write the following triads. Use whole notes.

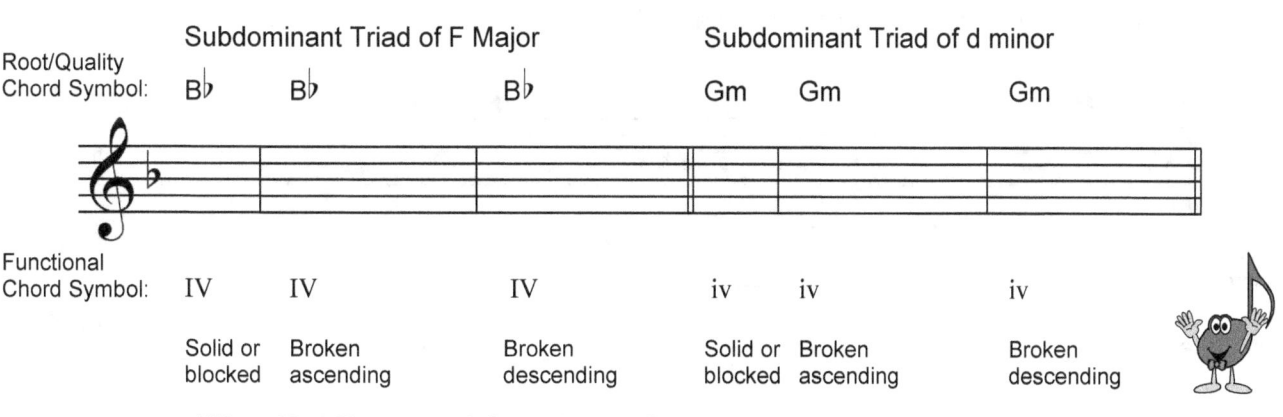

UltimateMusicTheory.com © Copyright 2017 Gloryland Publishing. All Rights Reserved.

FUNCTIONAL CHORD SYMBOLS - DOMINANT TRIADS in MAJOR and MINOR KEYS
(Use after Basic Rudiments Page 88)

The triad built on Scale Degree $\hat{5}$ of the Major scale is called the **Dominant** Triad. It is a Major triad. The **Functional Chord Symbol** for the Major Dominant Triad is V.

The triad built on Scale Degree $\hat{5}$ of the harmonic minor scale is called the **Dominant** Triad. It is a Major triad. The **Functional Chord Symbol** for the Major Dominant Triad is V.

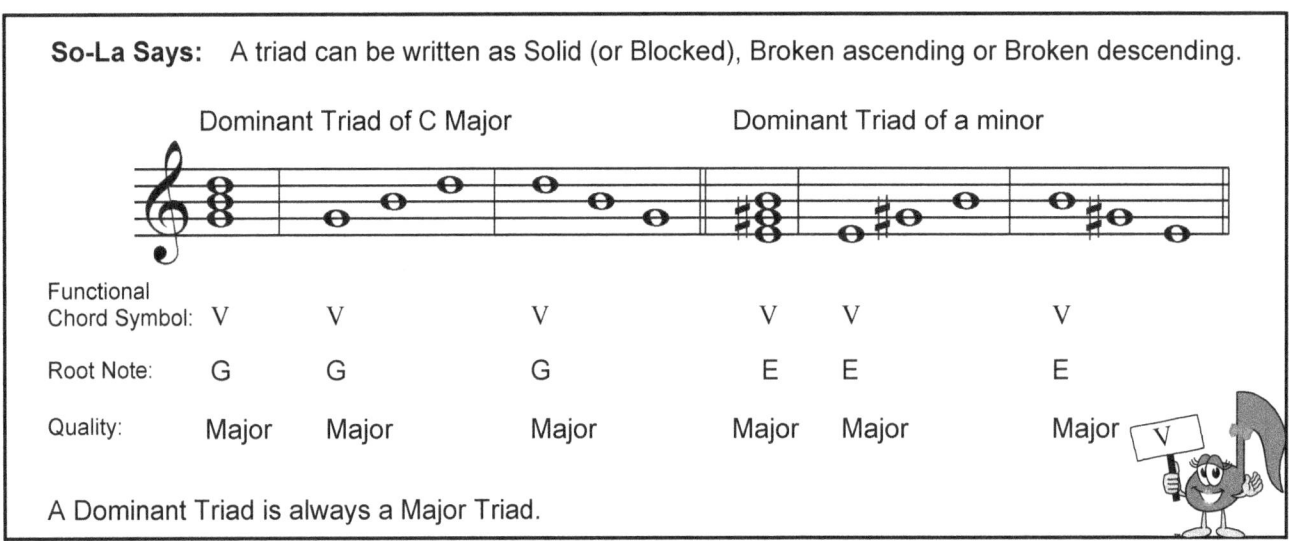

♫ **Ti-Do Tip:** The Dominant Triad of the minor key will have an accidental for the raised 7th (Leading Tone).

1. a) Name the Major key.
   b) Identify the Functional Chord Symbol for each triad.

Functional
Chord Symbol: _____   _____   _____   _____   _____   _____

Major key: _____   Major key: _____   Major key: _____

2. a) Name the minor key.
   b) Identify the Functional Chord Symbol for each triad.

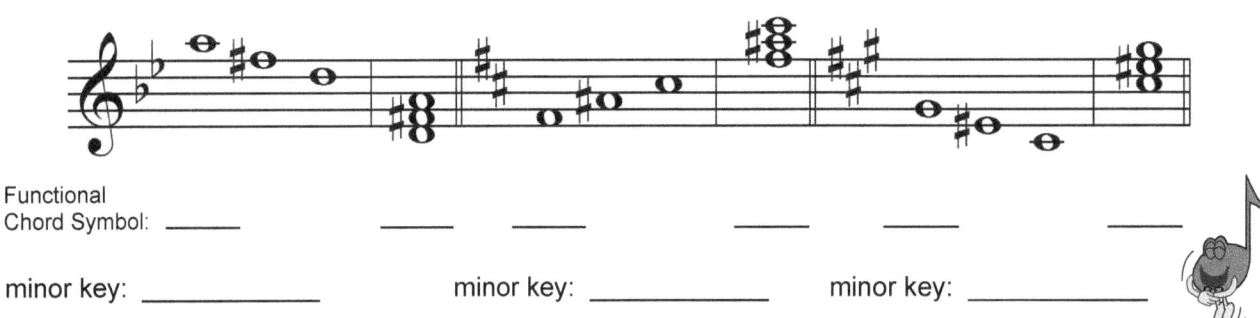

Functional
Chord Symbol: _____   _____   _____   _____   _____   _____

minor key: _____   minor key: _____   minor key: _____

ROOT/QUALITY CHORD SYMBOLS - DOMINANT TRIADS in MAJOR and MINOR KEYS
(Use after Basic Rudiments Page 88)

Root/Quality Chord Symbols are Letter Names that indicate the quality (Major or minor) of a triad.

An upper case letter indicates a Major triad. (Example: D = D Major triad)
The Dominant Triad is always a Major triad. An accidental will be needed in the minor key.

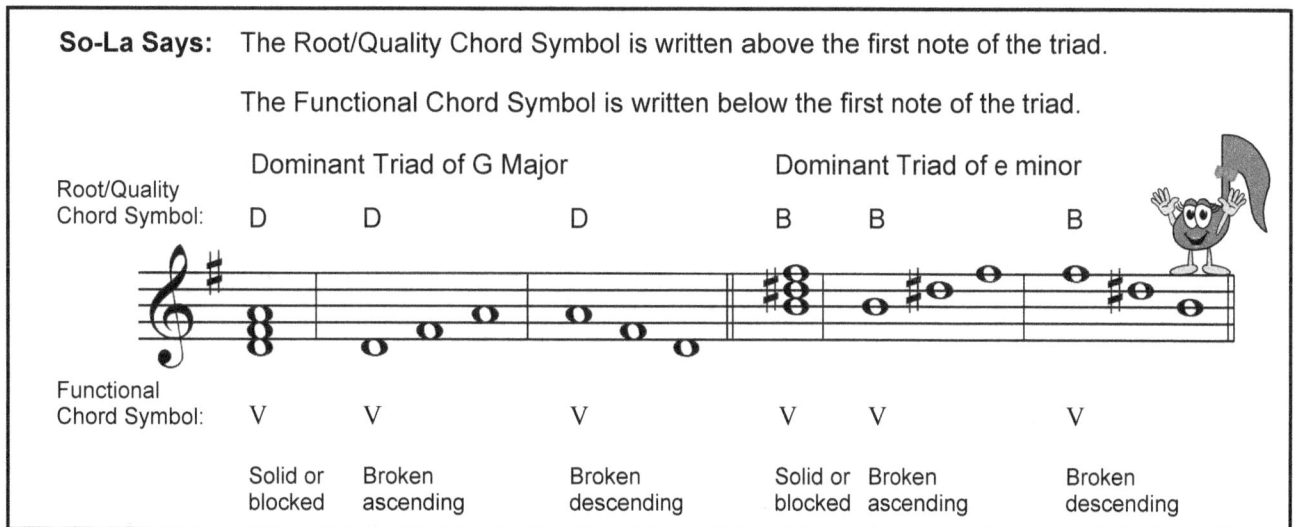

So-La Says: The Root/Quality Chord Symbol is written above the first note of the triad.

The Functional Chord Symbol is written below the first note of the triad.

♫ **Ti-Do Tip:** The Dominant Triad of a Major key is a Major triad. The Dominant Triad of a minor key is a Major triad because of the raised seventh note of the harmonic minor scale.

1. a) Name the Root/Quality Chord Symbol above each triad.
   b) Identify the Functional Chord Symbol below each triad.

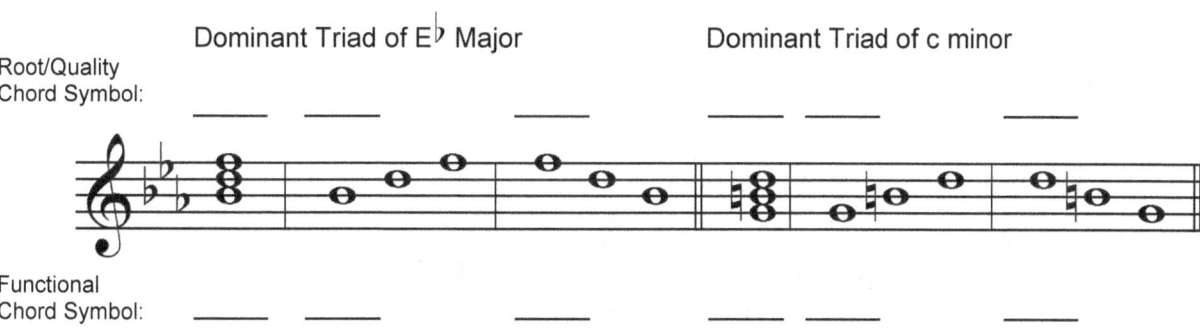

2. Write the following triads. Use whole notes.

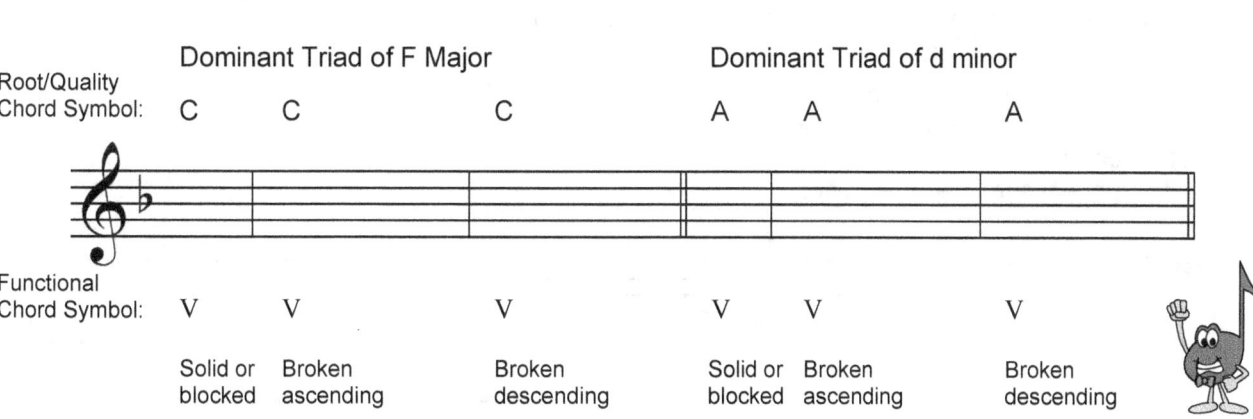

FUNCTIONAL CHORD SYMBOLS REVIEW (Use after Basic Rudiments Page 90)

Functional Chord Symbols are one way to symbolize chords. Functional Chord Symbols use Roman Numerals to show the scale degree on which the triad is built and the quality (Major or minor) of the triad.

So-La Says:	Major Triad = Upper case Roman Numeral; minor Triad = Lower case Roman Numeral		
	Triad Scale Degree	**Major Scale**	**Harmonic minor Scale**
	Tonic Triad	I	i
	Subdominant Triad	IV	iv
	Dominant Triad	V	V

1. Write the following solid (blocked) triads. Use whole notes. Use a Key Signature and any necessary accidentals. Write the Functional Chord Symbol below each triad.

    a) The Tonic triad of f sharp minor
    b) The Dominant triad of E flat Major
    c) The Subdominant triad of b minor
    d) The Dominant triad of g minor

2. Write the following broken ascending triads. Use whole notes. Use accidentals.
   Write the Functional Chord Symbol below each triad.

    a) The Tonic triad of A Major
    b) The Subdominant triad of B flat Major
    c) The Dominant triad of c minor
    d) The Subdominant triad of e minor

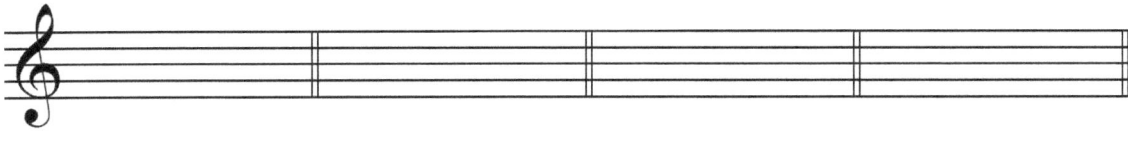

3. Write the following broken descending triads. Use whole notes. Use accidentals.
   Write the Functional Chord Symbol below each triad.

    a) The Dominant triad of a minor
    b) The Subdominant triad of C Major
    c) The Tonic triad of D Major
    d) The Subdominant triad of d minor

ROOT/QUALITY CHORD SYMBOLS REVIEW (Use after Basic Rudiments Page 90)

Root/Quality Chord Symbols are another way to symbolize chords. Root/Quality Chord Symbols use an upper case letter to indicate the Root of the Triad.

> **So-La Says:** Major Triad = Root of the Triad, written using an upper case letter.
> For Example: **C** = C Major Triad
>
> Minor Triad = Root of the Triad, written using an upper case letter with an "m" for minor.
> For Example: **Cm** = c minor Triad
>
> Root/Quality Chord Symbols are written above the staff.

1. Write the following solid (blocked) Tonic triads that match each Root/Quality Chord Symbol. Use whole notes. Use a Key Signature and any necessary accidentals. Name the key.

   E♭   Bm   Gm   G

   Key: _____   _____   _____   _____

2. Write the following solid (blocked) Subdominant triads that match each Root/Quality Chord Symbol. Use whole notes. Use a Key Signature and any necessary accidentals. Name the key.

   G   Fm   Bm   B♭

   Key: _____   _____   _____   _____

3. Write the following solid (blocked) Dominant triads that match each Root/Quality Chord Symbol. Use whole notes. Use accidentals. Name the Major key and the minor key for each triad.

   E   A   G   D

   Major key: _____   _____   _____   _____

   minor key: _____   _____   _____   _____

> ♪ **Ti-Do Time:** LISTEN as your Teacher plays the triads on Page 32 and Page 33.
> Identify if the triad played is a Major triad or a minor triad.

CONDUCTING in DUPLE TIME and BAR LINE REVIEWS (Use after Basic Rudiments Page 104)

A Conductor is a person who directs an orchestra, chorus or opera production. The Conductor keeps the musicians together by beating the pulse of the music with a baton (a stick) or sometimes with his/her hands.

The first beat of a measure is always down (the downbeat); the last beat is always up (the upbeat).

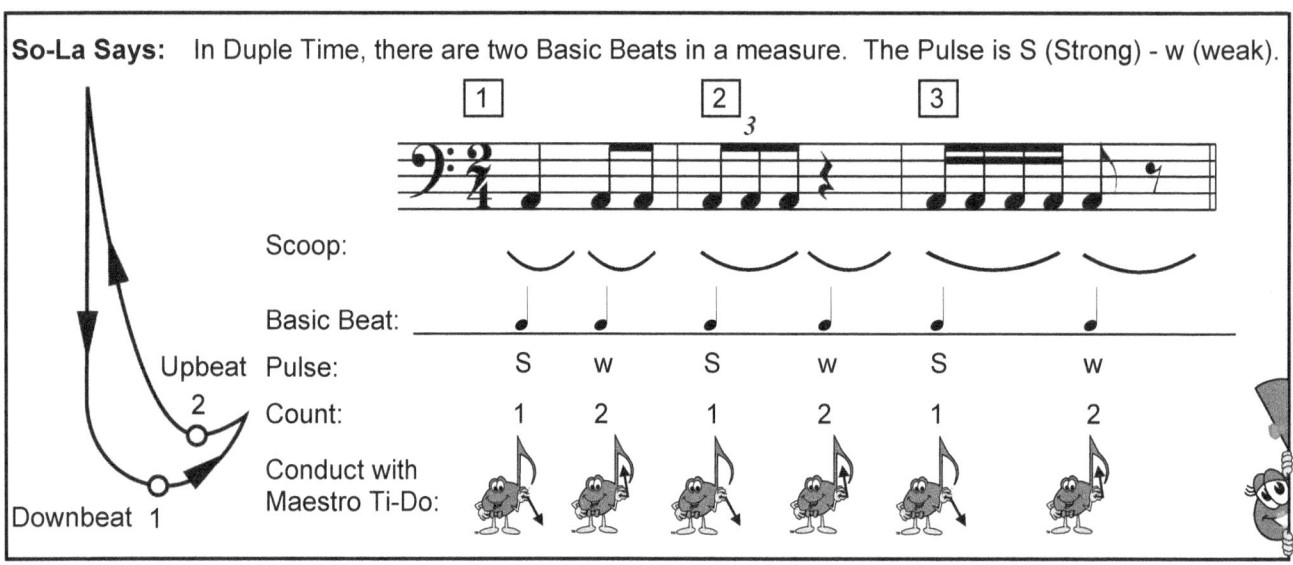

1. a) Based on the Time Signature, add Bar Lines to complete the following rhythms.
   b) Scoop each Basic Beat. Write the Basic Beat and the Pulse below each measure.

♫ Ti-Do Time:
1. TAP the Basic Beat with your foot while you CLAP each rhythm.
2. CONDUCT each rhythm while counting the beats.
3. CONDUCT each rhythm while speaking the Pulse: Strong - weak.

CONDUCTING in TRIPLE TIME and BAR LINE REVIEWS (Use after Basic Rudiments Page 105)

An **Anacrusis**, **Pickup** or **Upbeat** is a note or group of notes (or rests) in the first incomplete measure at the beginning of the music. The last (final) measure at the end of the music will also be an incomplete measure. Together they equal one complete measure. The strong beat is the downbeat, the first beat in the measure.

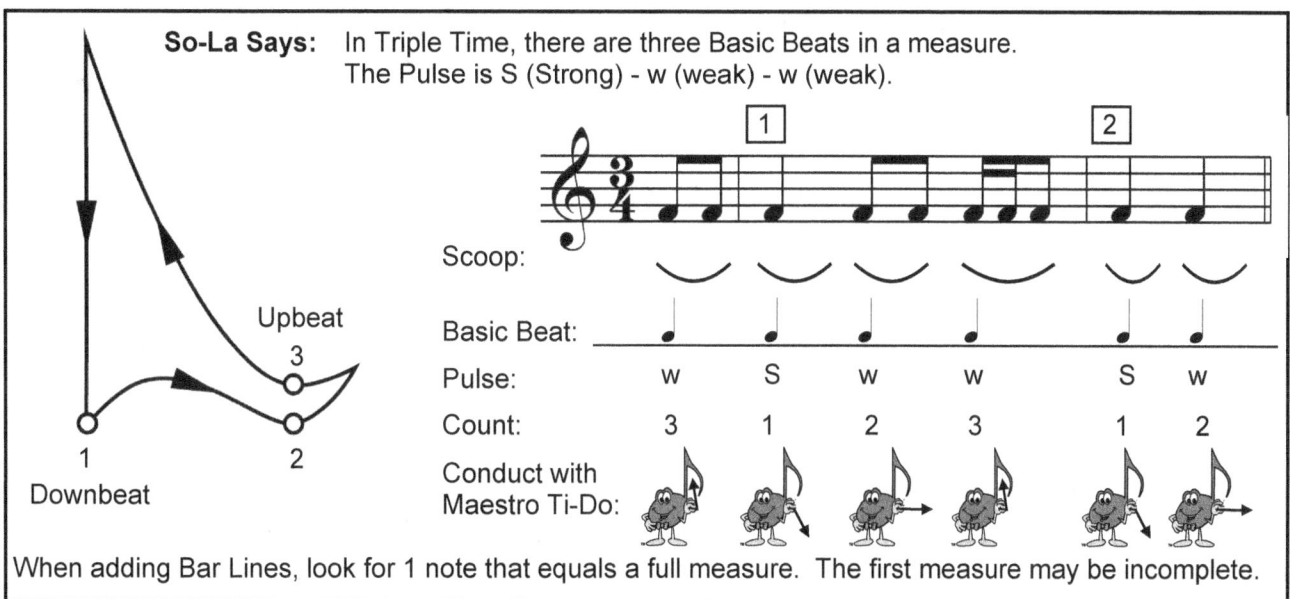

When adding Bar Lines, look for 1 note that equals a full measure. The first measure may be incomplete.

1. a) Based on the Time Signature, add Bar Lines to complete the following rhythms.
   b) Scoop each Basic Beat. Write the Basic Beat and the Pulse below each measure.

♪ Ti-Do Time:
1. TAP the Basic Beat with your foot while you CLAP each rhythm.
2. CONDUCT each rhythm while counting the beats.
3. CONDUCT each rhythm while speaking the Pulse: Strong - weak - weak.

UltimateMusicTheory.com © Copyright 2017 Gloryland Publishing. All Rights Reserved.

CONDUCTING in QUADRUPLE TIME and BAR LINE REVIEWS (Use after Basic Rudiments Page 105)

The **Conducting Pattern** is the same for all Duple Time Signatures (top number = 2), for all Triple Time Signatures (top number = 3) and for all Quadruple Time Signatures (top number = 4).

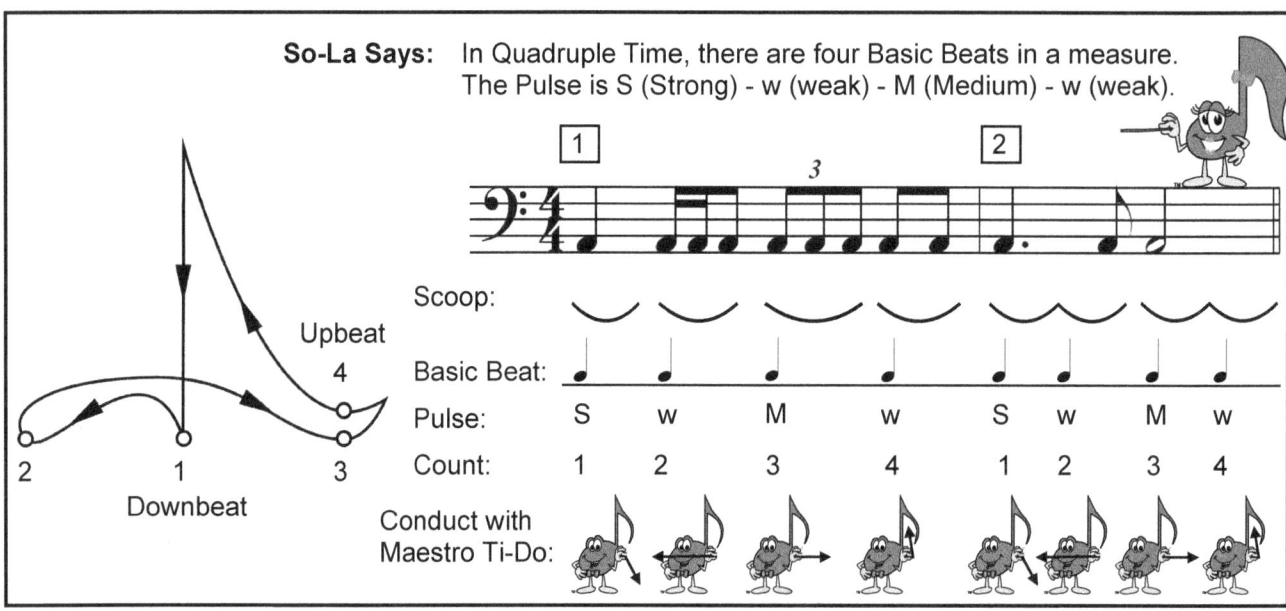

1. a) Based on the Time Signature, add Bar Lines to complete the following rhythms.
   b) Scoop each Basic Beat. Write the Basic Beat and the Pulse below each measure.

JOINING BEAMS and ADDING RESTS REVIEW (Use after Basic Rudiments Page 110)

When the bottom number of the Time Signature is a "4", the Basic Beat is a quarter note.
When the bottom number of the Time Signature is an "8", the Basic Beat is an eighth note.

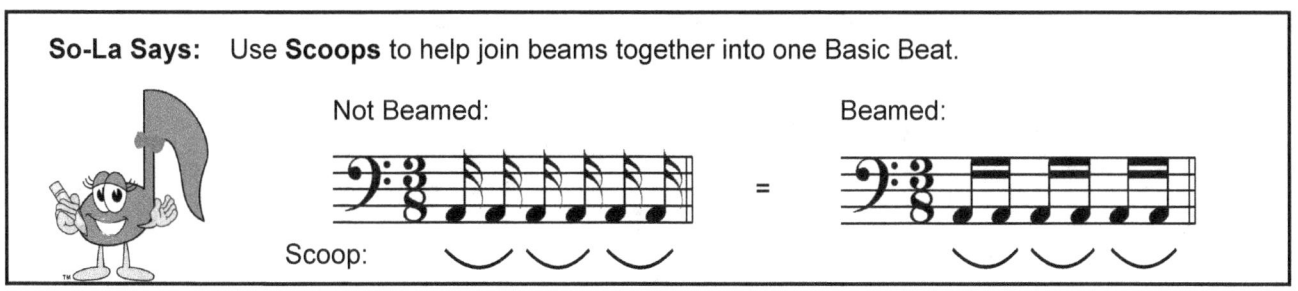

So-La Says: Use **Scoops** to help join beams together into one Basic Beat.

1. a) In line 1, scoop each eighth note Basic Beat.
   b) Rewrite each rhythm in the measure below in line 2, beaming the notes into Basic Beats.
   c) In line 2, scoop each eighth note Basic Beat.

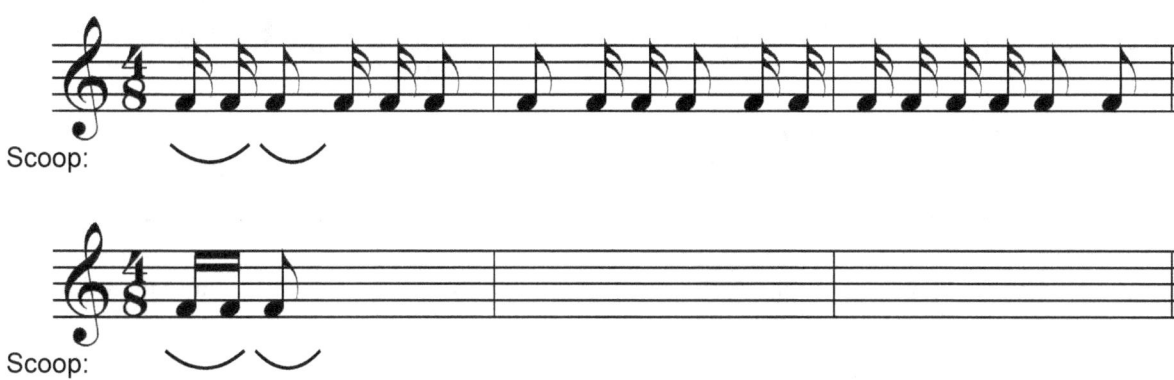

♪ **Ti-Do Tip:** Before adding rests, determine if the Basic Beat is an eighth note or a quarter note. The bottom number of the Time Signature determines the value of the Basic Beat.

2. a) Scoop each Basic Beat. Write the Basic Beat and the pulse below each measure.
   b) Add rests below each bracket to complete each measure.

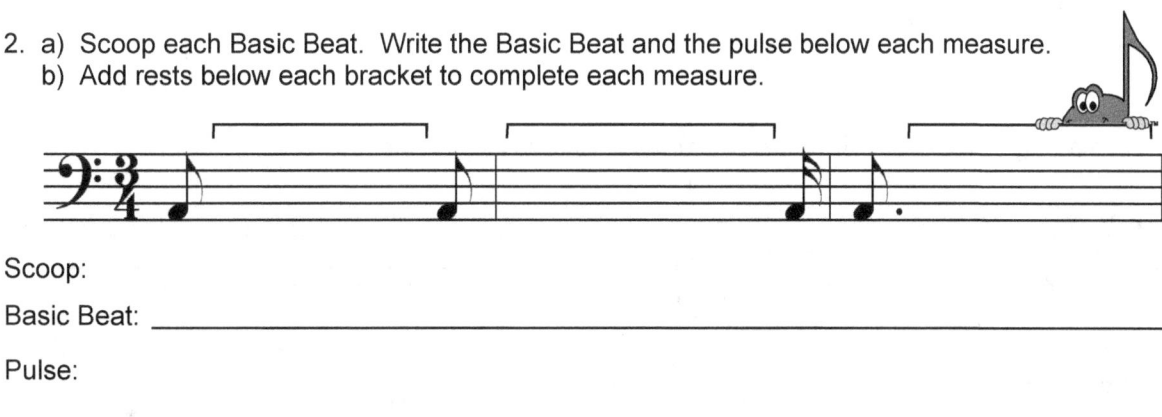

Scoop:

Basic Beat: _____

Pulse:

Scoop:

Basic Beat: _____

Pulse:

TRANSPOSITION - ONE OCTAVE - CHANGE OF CLEF (Use after Basic Rudiments Page 124)

A melody may be transposed up or down one octave in the same clef or **transposed with a change of clef**.

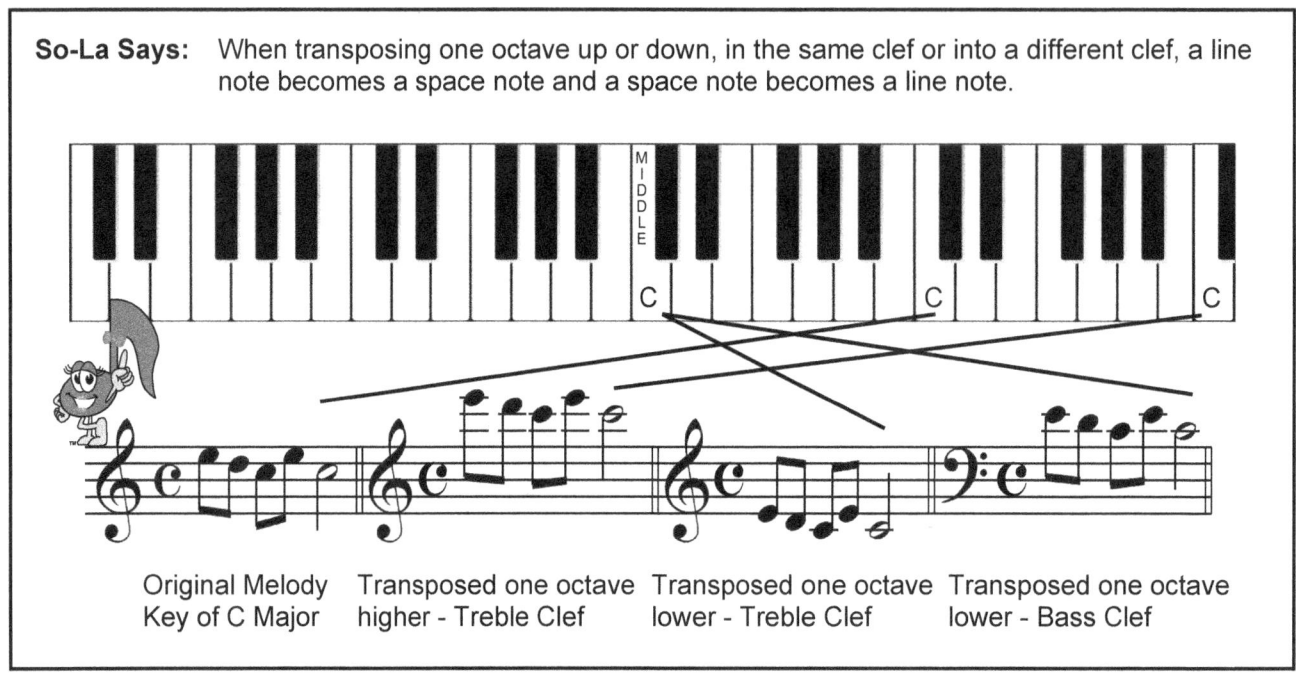

So-La Says: When transposing one octave up or down, in the same clef or into a different clef, a line note becomes a space note and a space note becomes a line note.

Original Melody Key of C Major — Transposed one octave higher - Treble Clef — Transposed one octave lower - Treble Clef — Transposed one octave lower - Bass Clef

♪ **Ti-Do Tip:** Write the Clef sign, Key Signature and Time Signature. Use appropriate stem directions.

1. Name the Major key. Transpose the melody up one octave into the Treble Clef.

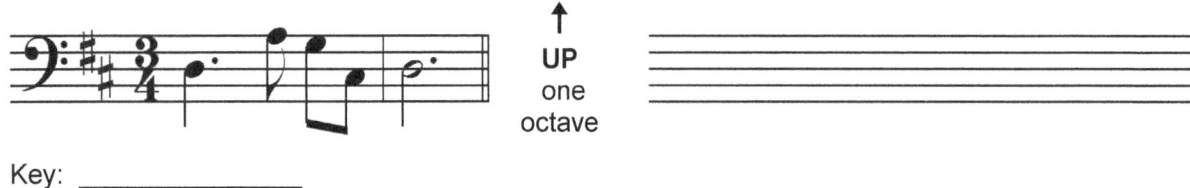

↑ **UP** one octave

Key: _____

2. Name the Major key. Transpose the melody down one octave into the Bass Clef.

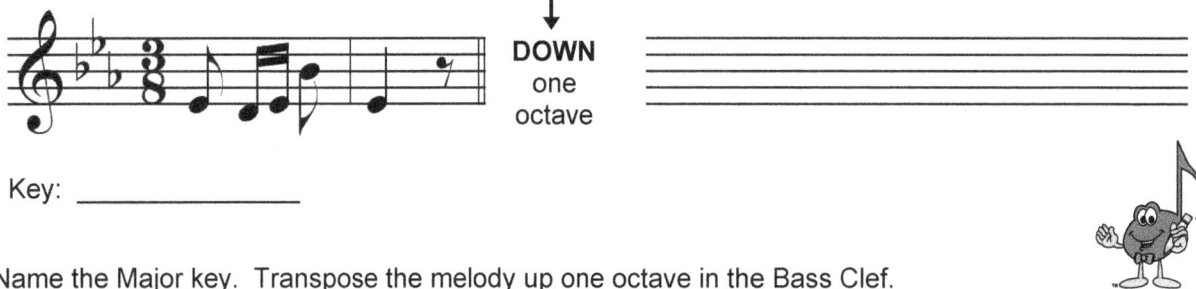

↓ **DOWN** one octave

Key: _____

3. Name the Major key. Transpose the melody up one octave in the Bass Clef.

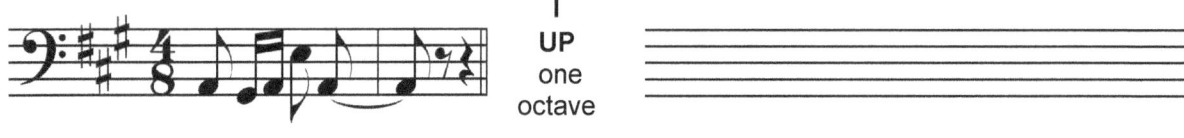

↑ **UP** one octave

Key: _____

TRANSPOSITION - SAME CLEF or CHANGE OF CLEF (Use after Basic Rudiments Page 124)

When transposing a melody in the **same clef or in a change of clef**, all notation must be rewritten. Write the bar lines in first. Use a ruler. Write the tempo, dynamics and articulation markings when given.

1. Name the Major key. Transpose the melody down one octave into the Bass Clef.

Key: _____

2. Name the Major key. Transpose the melody up one octave into the Treble Clef.

Key: _____

3. Name the Major key. Transpose the melody down one octave in the Treble Clef.

Key: _____

ANALYSIS of MELODY - MELODIC MOTIVE (Use after Basic Rudiments Page 124)

A melody has a **melodic motive** which may be repeated (repetition) or altered (imitation) to create a phrase.

> **So-La Says:** A melody may have a repeated melodic motive in the same clef or in a different clef.
>
> **Repetition** - when a motive is repeated by the same voice at the same pitch in the same clef.
>
> **Imitation** - when a motive is repeated (exact or varied) by another voice at the same pitch or at a different pitch. The imitation may be in the same clef or in a different clef.
>
> **Polyphony** - when music contains two or more independent melodic lines.

French composer Jean-Philippe Rameau (late Baroque period) used both repetition and imitation in his composition Frère Jacques. Imitation (musical counterpoint) is used in Baroque inventions and canons. The piece below is a 2-voice round. Voice 1 is in the Treble Staff. Voice 2 is in the Bass Staff.

The motive is written in Measure 1. In Measure 2, the notes are written again at the same pitch in the same clef. This is Repetition (same voice, same note names, same intervals, same pitch).

The motive is written in Measure 1. In Measure 3, the notes are written at a different voice/octave/pitch. This is Imitation (same note names and intervals, different voice, different pitch - one octave lower).

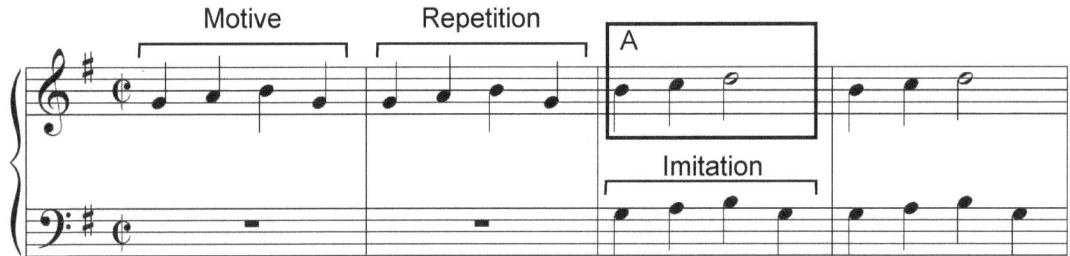

1. Analyze the melody above (variation on Frère Jacques), by answering the questions below.

    a) Circle if the R.H. motive at letter A is repeated in the R.H. measure 4 as: repetition   or   imitation.

    b) Circle if the R.H. motive at letter A is repeated in the L.H. measure 5 as: repetition   or   imitation.

    c) Circle if the RH motive at letter B is repeated in the R.H. measure 6 as: repetition   or   imitation.

    d) Circle if the rhythm at letter B and the rhythm in the L.H. measure 7 is: same   or   different.

ANALYSIS of MELODY - MELODIC PHRASE (Use after Basic Rudiments Page 124)

A melody has a motive (short musical idea) which may be repeated or altered to create a **melodic phrase**, usually 2 - 4 measures or more. A melody may repeat a phrase in the same, similar or different manner.

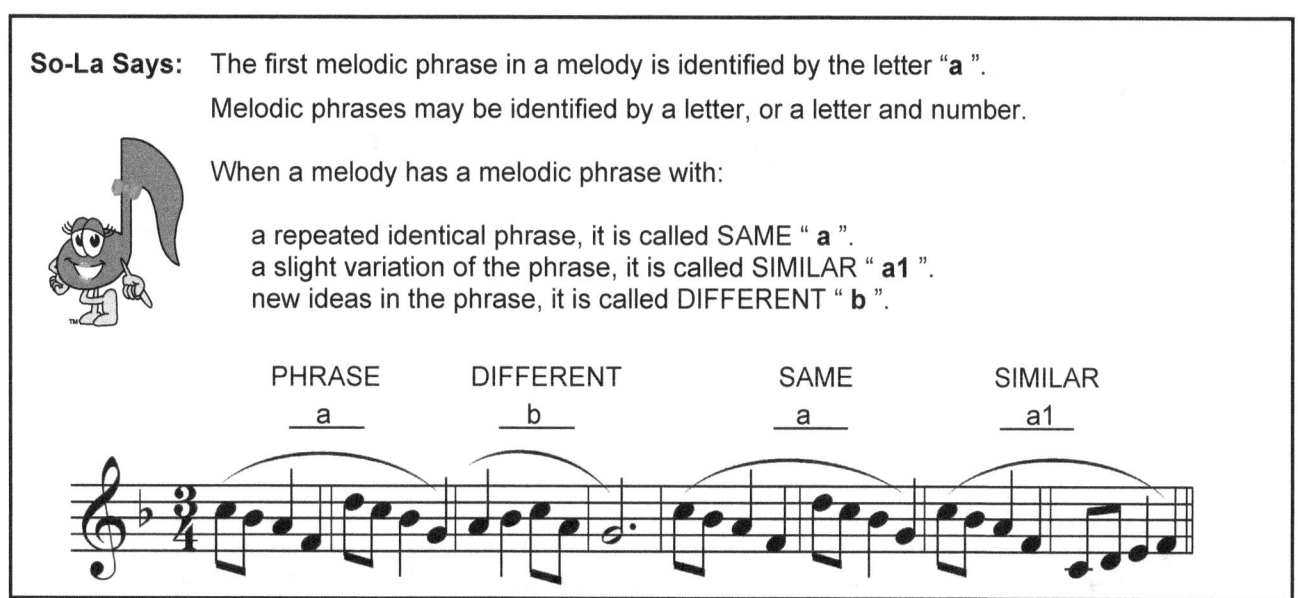

♫ **Ti-Do Tip:** A melody may repeat the same phrase (a), or have a similar phrase (a1), or have a different phrase (b) that creates a series of melodic phrases within a piece of music.

1. Identify each of the melodic phrases as: a (same), a1 (similar), or b (different).

ANALYSIS of COMPOSITION - IDENTIFICATION OF SECTIONS (Use after Basic Rudiments Page 139)

Melodic phrases are combined to create a complete composition. A **composition** may be divided into "part forms" called **sections**. A composition may have a one-part form, two-part form, three-part form, etc.

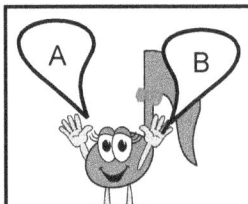 **So-La Says:** A Composition in two-part form is called Binary Form.

Each section or part is identified as "**A**" and "**B**" (upper case letters). Melodic phrases within each section of A and B are identified as: a, a1, or b (lower case letters).

♫ **Ti-Do Tip:** In the two-part form (AB), each part is contrasting (different). A motive may be common to both parts. Binary form was popular in the Baroque period (1600 - 1750).

1. Analyze the music in C Major by answering the questions below.

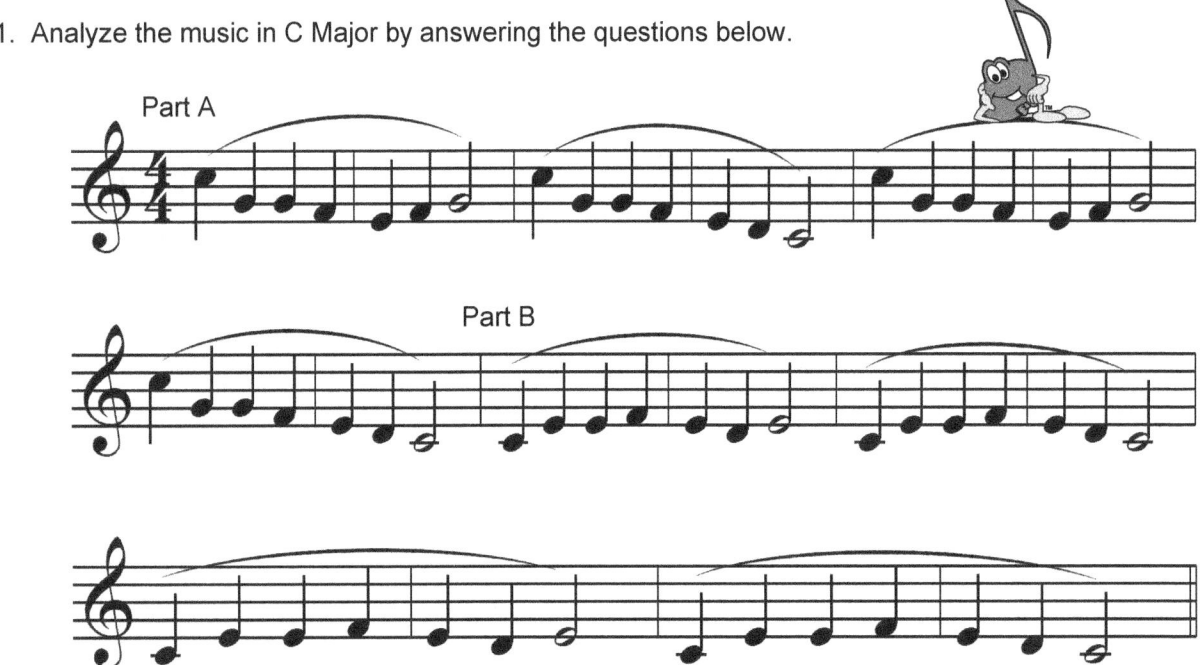

a) Circle if the number of phrases in Part A of the two-part form is: two or four or eight.

b) Circle if the phrase ending in measure 8 is: a stable scale degree or an unstable scale degree.

c) Circle if the 1st melodic phrase and 2nd melodic phrase are: same (a) or similar (a1) or different (b).

d) Circle if the number of phrases in Part B of the two-part form is: two or four or eight.

e) Circle if the phrase ending in measure 10 is: a stable scale degree or an unstable scale degree.

f) Circle if the 1st melodic phrase and 5th melodic phrase are: same (a) or similar (a1) or different (b).

g) Circle if the rhythmic pattern in Part A and Part B are: same or different.

ANALYSIS of COMPOSITION - MOTIVE, PHRASE and SECTION (Use after Basic Rudiments Page 139)

A **Composition** begins with a motive (idea) to create a phrase (sentence) that develops a section (story). Analysis of composition helps us discover how the music (story) unfolds and leads us through the adventure.

> **So-La Says:** Analysis of Composition is discovering and learning about the:
>
> **Motive** - a musical idea (2 - 7 notes or more), a short melodic and/or rhythmic fragment, a building block.
> **Motive pattern** - a motive may be repeated as repetition, same rhythmic and/or melodic pattern.
>
> **Phrase** - a musical sentence (2 - 4 measures or more), ends on a stable ($\hat{1}$ or $\hat{3}$) or unstable ($\hat{2}$ or $\hat{7}$) degree.
> **Phrase pattern** - a melodic phrase may be repeated as same (a), similar (a1) or different (b).
>
> **Section** - a musical group (2 - 4 phrases or more) creating/unfolding the musical story, dance, piece, etc.
> **Section pattern** - a section may be repeated and identified as a part form. (AB), (ABA), (ABACA) etc.

♫ **Ti-Do Tip:** Play the music on your instrument.

1. Analyze the music in C Major by answering the questions below.

    a) Identify the Parts directly above the first phrase and above the third phrase as Part A or as Part B.

    b) Circle if the number of phrases in Part A in this two-part form piece is: two or four or eight.

    c) Circle if the rhythmic pattern in measure 1 and in measure 2 is: same or different.

    d) Circle if the number of measures in this two-part form piece is: 15 or 16 or 17.

    e) Circle if the scale degree ending the 1st phrase is the: Tonic or Subdominant or Dominant.

    f) Circle if the 3rd and 4th melodic phrases are: same (a) or similar (a1) or different (b).

    g) Circle if the rhythmic pattern in Part A and in Part B is: same or different.

COMPOSITION - ENDING on a STABLE SCALE DEGREE (Use after Basic Rudiments Page 139)

A **composition** (or melody) creates a melodic phrase that ends on a **stable scale degree**. A melody ending on the Tonic note (stable degree $\hat{1}$) or the Mediant note (stable degree $\hat{3}$) sounds finished (the end).

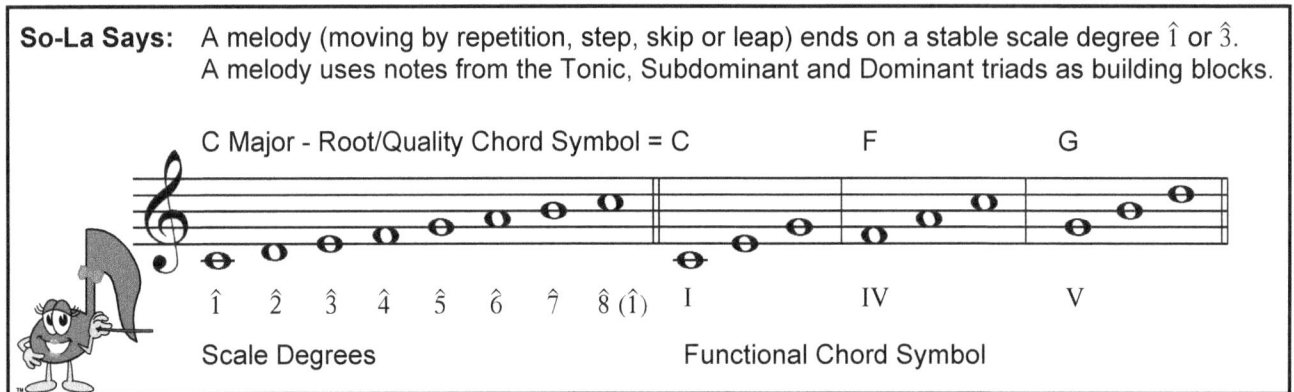

So-La Says: A melody (moving by repetition, step, skip or leap) ends on a stable scale degree $\hat{1}$ or $\hat{3}$.
A melody uses notes from the Tonic, Subdominant and Dominant triads as building blocks.

♪ **Ti-Do Tip:** Non-triad notes, called Passing Tones (pt), are used to connect Triad Tones with stepwise motion in the same direction. For example, in measure 1 of the question in C Major below, D is a passing tone between chord tones C and E of the C Major Tonic Triad (C E G).

1. Complete the four measure melodies. Observe the Key Signature and the Time Signature.

   a) Observing the Root/Quality Chord Symbols, use notes that move by repetition, step, skip or leap within each given Triad. Use the given rhythm. End each melody on a stable degree $\hat{1}$ or $\hat{3}$.
   b) Draw a double bar line at the end of each four measure melody.
   c) Label the Functional Chord Symbols below each measure.

COMPOSITION - FOUR MEASURE MELODY (Use after Basic Rudiments Page 139)

Music is sound. **Composition** (or melody writing) begins by exploring the elements of music. Compose a melody and then sing or play it on a keyboard or other instrument until you can hear the music in your head.

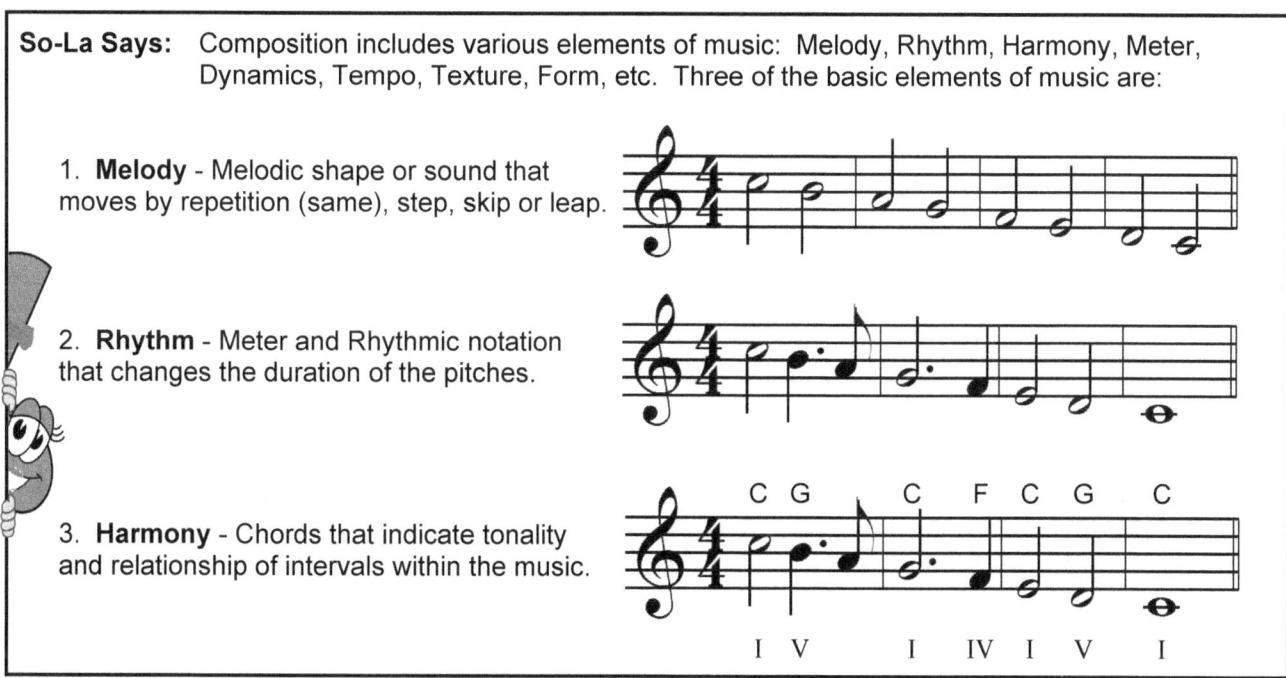

So-La Says: Composition includes various elements of music: Melody, Rhythm, Harmony, Meter, Dynamics, Tempo, Texture, Form, etc. Three of the basic elements of music are:

1. **Melody** - Melodic shape or sound that moves by repetition (same), step, skip or leap.

2. **Rhythm** - Meter and Rhythmic notation that changes the duration of the pitches.

3. **Harmony** - Chords that indicate tonality and relationship of intervals within the music.

1. Compose 3 four measure melodies. Observe the Key Signature. Draw a double bar line at the end.

   a) Melody - Create a melodic shape moving by same, step, skip or leap. End on a stable degree $\hat{1}$ or $\hat{3}$.
   b) Rhythm - Observe the Time Signature. Use correct rhythmic notation in each measure.
   c) Harmony - Add Root/Quality Chord Symbols above each measure to indicate harmony.

♪ **Ti-Do Tip:** Play your 3 compositions. Listen to the melody, rhythm and harmony.

IMAGINE, COMPOSE, EXPLORE (Use after Basic Rudiments Page 139)

♪ **I**magine the music telling a story or an idea. The title describes the composition.
♪ **C**ompose your musical idea. The name (top right) identifies the composer.
♪ **E**xplore the music. Add "So-La Sparkles" (terms & signs) to enhance the sound.

So-La Says: 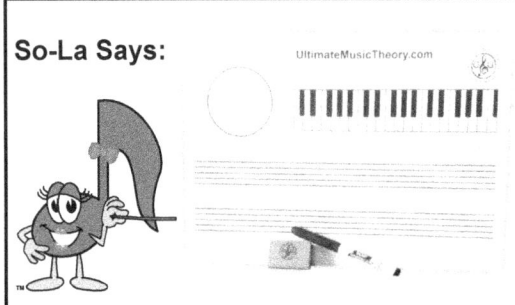 **Composing** means to create music. Use your imagination to compose. Record yourself and use it as a reference to write your melody on the Ultimate Whiteboard.

On the Whiteboard, use different ideas (articulation, dynamics) to create different sounds. Play your melody again.

Write the final copy from your Whiteboard into your Workbook.

1. For each of the following: compose a melody in measures 2, 3 and 4. Use your own rhythm.

    a) Imagine your musical idea by completing the title at the top. Write your name as the composer.
    b) Compose a melody in the given Key Signature and Time Signature. End on a stable degree $\hat{1}$ or $\hat{3}$.
    c) Explore the music. Add "So-La Sparkles" using dynamics, articulation, terms, etc. Mark the phrases.

A Musical Bowl of _____
(title)

Key: A Major

_____
(composer)

A _____ **Sandwich**
(title)

Key: C Major

_____
(composer)

 ♫ **Ti-Do Time:** Get your "Composers Certificate". SCAN your composition (on this page) and send it to us at: info@ultimatemusictheory.com and we will send you a special **Ultimate Music Theory Composers Certificate** - FREE.

UltimateMusicTheory.com © Copyright 2017 Gloryland Publishing. All Rights Reserved.

ANALYSIS and SIGHT READING (Use after Basic Rudiments Page 139)

1. Analyze the music by answering the questions below. Play (Sight Read) the piece "Funny Ferret".

   a) Name the Major key. _____   Name the scale degree at the letter A. _____

   b) Circle an ascending Major scale directly on the music. Name the Major scale. _____

   c) Circle the number of beats given to the combined tied notes at the letter B: 4 or 6 or 10.

   d) Circle if the R.H. phrases at mm. 5 - 6 and mm. 7 - 8 are: same (a) or similar (a1) or different.

   e) Explain the term accel. in measure 7. _____

   f) Circle if the descending scale at the letter D is: Major or harmonic minor or chromatic.

   g) Circle if the triad at the letter E is the: Tonic triad or Subdominant triad or Dominant triad.

   h) Circle the number of slurs that are in the piece "Funny Ferret": 6 or 7 or 8.

MUSIC HISTORY - THE ORCHESTRA - FAMILIES and INSTRUMENTS

An Orchestra is a large group of musicians performing together on String, Woodwind, Brass, Percussion and other instruments. The **Orchestral Instruments** are divided into sections or "families". The first 4 instruments listed below in the String, Woodwind & Brass Family are ordered from highest to lowest pitch.

String Family: violin, viola, cello & double bass (bowed or plucked). The harp (plucked) is also a string instrument.

Woodwind Family: flute, oboe, clarinet, bassoon, cor anglais (English horn), contrabassoon & saxophone.

Brass Family: trumpet, French horn, trombone & tuba.

Percussion Family: Pitched: timpani, glockenspiel, celesta, xylophone, tubular bells, etc.
Unpitched: snare drum, bass drum, tambourine, gong, triangle, cymbals, castanet, blocks, maraca, bongo, etc.

Other Instruments: include piano & glass harmonica.

Instruments in the String Family are made of wood or metal, and have strings. The strings may be bowed or plucked as they vibrate and create sound. Shorter strings = higher sound; longer strings = lower sound. The hollow body of the String instrument acts as a resonator to control the dynamics.

1. Name 2 instruments in the String Family. _____

Instruments in the Woodwind Family are divided into 2 main sections: In section one, players blow across the tip of a tube. In section two, players blow into 1 or more reeds (thin strips of cane). Woodwind instruments may be made from wood or they may be made from clay, metal, glass, ivory or plastics.

2. Name 2 instruments in the Woodwind Family. _____

Instruments in the Brass Family create sound when the player blows into a funnel-shaped mouthpiece or cup. The way the player vibrates their lips against the mouthpiece is called their "embouchure". Brass instruments are made from metal tubes with the mouthpiece at one end, widening to a "bell" at the other.

3. Name 2 instruments in the Brass Family. _____

Instruments in the Percussion Family create sound when they are hit, scraped, rubbed, shaken or whirled. This is the largest family of instruments. They range in size from tiny sleigh bells to huge bells. Percussion instruments are classified as those with: definite pitch ("pitched") and indefinite pitch ("unpitched").

4. Name 2 instruments in the Percussion Family. _____

Instruments in the "Other" Family are instruments that do not create sound using the definitions of the four main Instrument Families.

5. Name 2 instruments in the "Other" Family. _____

ORGANIZE THE ORCHESTRA!

1. Name the correct Orchestra Section for each instrument: String, Woodwind, Brass, Percussion or Other.

The Violin is in the _____ Orchestra Section.

The Flute is in the _____ Orchestra Section.

The Triangle is in the _____ Orchestra Section.

The Clarinet is in the _____ Orchestra Section.

The Cello is in the _____ Orchestra Section.

The Snare Drum is in the _____ Orchestra Section.

The French Horn is in the _____ Orchestra Section.

The Bass Drum is in the _____ Orchestra Section.

The Piano is in the _____ Orchestra Section.

The Tuba is in the _____ Orchestra Section.

The Timpani is in the _____ Orchestra Section.

The Bassoon is in the _____ Orchestra Section.

The Harp is in the _____ Orchestra Section.

The Viola is in the _____ Orchestra Section.

The Trombone is in the _____ Orchestra Section.

MUSIC APPRECIATION - MUSICAL INSTRUMENTS & VOICE - RANGE CHART

Each musical instrument and human voice has a specific range in pitch (lowest to highest note). The piano has a range of 88 keys, beginning with A_0 and B_0, followed by 7 octaves from C_1 to C_8. Middle C is C_4.

1. Based on the Instrument//Voice Range Chart below, answer the following questions.

    a) Name the string instrument whose range is below C_4. _____

    b) Name the woodwind instrument whose range is from C_4 to C_7. _____

    c) Name the brass instrument with the lowest range. _____

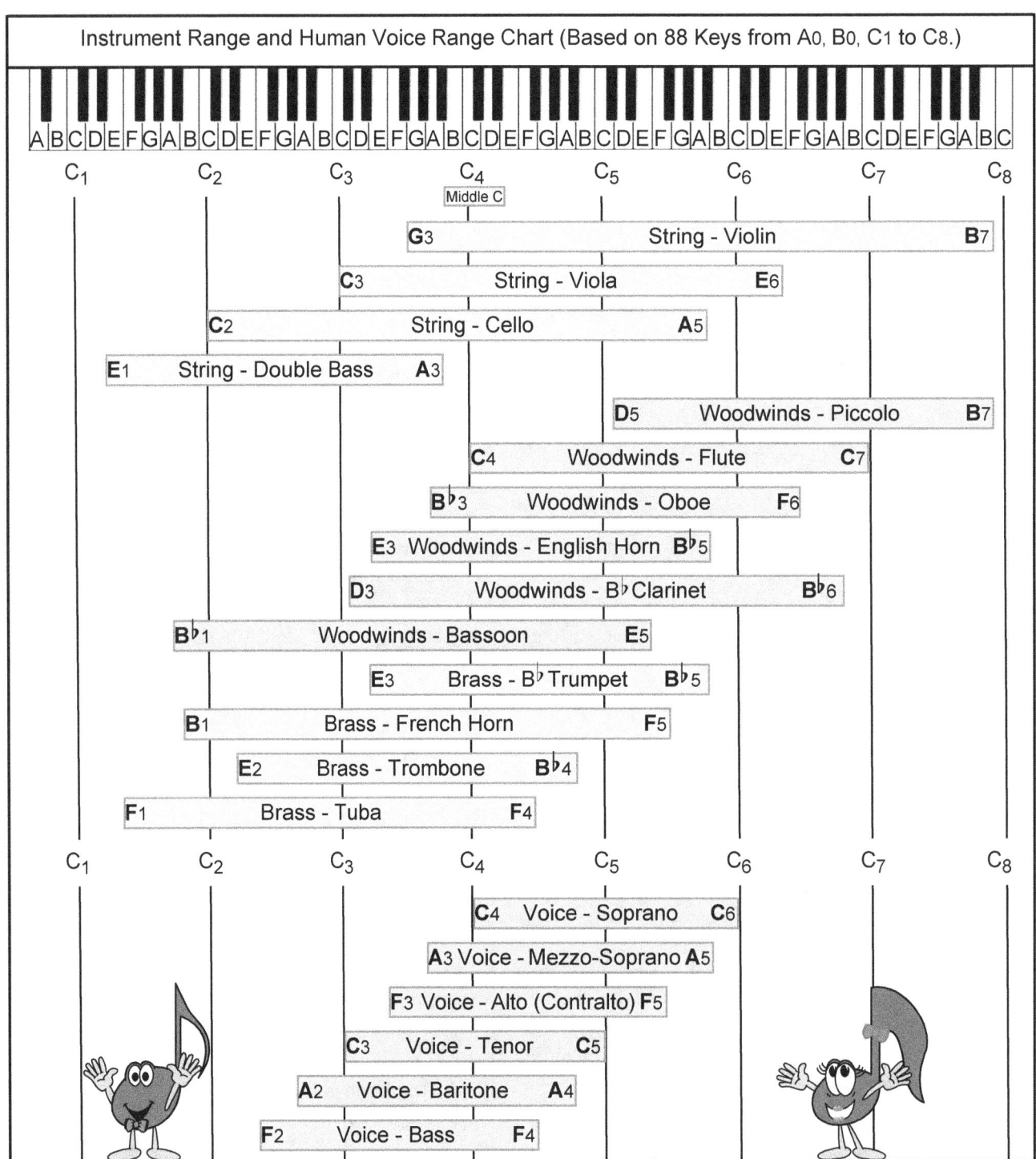

UltimateMusicTheory.com © Copyright 2017 Gloryland Publishing. All Rights Reserved.

MUSIC APPRECIATION - MUSICAL INSTRUMENTS - TONE COLOR OR TIMBRE

Each musical instrument produces a unique tone color or timbre that is defined by the sound characteristics of the instrument. Different instruments may play the same pitch (note) and use the same dynamic level while producing different tone colors of the fundamental note. The fundamental note is the note you read, play and hear. Overtones, heard with the fundamental note, create the characteristic sound quality.

A piano and a violin may play the same pitch, but because one is struck and one is bowed, their sounds are different.

The tone color of the instrument enables us to tell the difference just by listening to the sound.

Overtones are specific higher vibrations (or pitches) heard with the fundamental pitch (note). Overtones are generated naturally on acoustic instruments. The lower the register (range of notes) of the instrument, the "richer" the Tone Color because the ear can hear more of the overtones in the low notes. The higher the register, the fewer the overtones that can be heard by the human ear. Some are beyond human hearing!

So-La Says: Understanding the Tone Color or Timbre of the instruments of the orchestra is a necessary part of being a Composer. Tone Color creates sound effects.

Let's have fun! Pretend that you are using the Instruments of the Orchestra to create Sound Effects for a scene in a movie that Ti-Do wants to produce.

Think of the Tone Color (Timbre) of the different instruments and decide which instrument you think would match the scene!

1. Read the "Scene Description" and select which of the 2 instruments would have the Tone Color to match.

a) Scene 1: Thunder boomed and crashed across the darkened sky.

☐ Timpani ☐ Flute

b) Scene 2: The water trickled and shimmered in the light breeze.

☐ Tuba ☐ Harp

c) Scene 3: The soldiers marched in unison across the town square.

☐ Trumpet ☐ Triangle

♫ **Ti-Do Time:** Create your own scene with 2 instrument choices. Ask your parent or teacher to choose.

d) Scene 4: _____

☐ _____ ☐ _____

MUSIC HISTORY - BENJAMIN BRITTEN and HIS MUSIC

Benjamin Britten (1913 - 1976) was a great British composer, conductor and a remarkable musician. Britten wrote over 100 major works, including his first song cycle "Seven Sonnets of Michelangelo", for his partner (tenor singer) Peter Pears. Britten composed operas, string quartets, a violin concerto, choral works, symphonies and orchestral works including the **Young Person's Guide to the Orchestra**.

Britten's Young Person's Guide to the Orchestra (Op. 34), commissioned by the BBC in 1946, is a 16 minute work introducing various instruments and instrument families of the orchestra. The piece is based on the melodic theme from Baroque composer Henry Purcell's incidental music to the play Abdelazer.

The Outline of the **Young Person's Guide to the Orchestra** is:

Theme: An 8 measure theme in d minor is played six times to introduce the orchestra and its four main families: Woodwinds, Brass, Strings and Percussion.

Variations: 13 Variations, each featuring a different instrument (or combination).

Fugue: A fragment of Purcell's theme is played in imitation by each instrument (in the same order as in the variations).

Go to **GSGMUSIC.com** - For Easy Access to listening to the music Young Person's Guide to the Orchestra.

1. Listen to Britten's three part Young Person's Guide to the Orchestra: Theme, Variations and Fugue. Identify the instruments heard in each section. Check (✓) the correct answer to the questions below.

Theme: The Full (*tutti*) Orchestra plays the theme first and last. The order of instrument families playing is:

☐ Strings, Woodwinds, Percussion, Brass ☐ Woodwinds, Brass, Strings, Percussion

---

Variation 1: The featured instruments playing their own *Presto* Variation are:

☐ Flute and Piccolo ☐ Trombone and Tuba

Variation 2: The featured instruments playing their own *Lento* Variation are:

☐ Violins ☐ Oboes

Variation 3: The featured instruments playing their own *Moderato* Variation are:

☐ Clarinets ☐ French Horns

Variation 4: The featured instrument(s) playing it's own *Allegro alla marcia* Variation is:

☐ Harp ☐ Bassoons

MUSIC APPRECIATION - YOUNG PERSON'S GUIDE to the ORCHESTRA - By BENJAMIN BRITTEN

Variation 5: The featured instruments playing their own *Brillante: alla polacca* Variation are:

☐ Violins ☐ Flutes

Variation 6: The featured instruments playing their own *Meno mosso* Variation are:

☐ Trumpets ☐ Violas

Variation 7: The featured instruments playing their own *deep rich* Variation are:

☐ Cellos ☐ Piccolos

Variation 8: The featured instruments playing the *lento ma poco a poco accel. al Allegro* Variation are:

☐ Double Basses ☐ Trumpets

Variation 9: The featured instrument(s) playing it's own *Maestoso* Variation is:

☐ Harp ☐ Bassoons

Variation 10: The featured instruments playing their own *L'istesso tempo* Variation are:

☐ Violas ☐ French Horns

Variation 11: The featured instruments playing their own *Vivace* Variation are:

☐ Trumpets ☐ Oboes

Variation 12: The featured instruments playing their own *Allegro* Variation are:

☐ Violins and Violas ☐ Trombones and Tuba

Variation 13: The featured instruments playing their own *Moderato* Variation are:

☐ Woodwinds: flute, oboe, *tutti* ☐ Percussion: Timpani, Bass Drum, Cymbals, *tutti*

Fugue: The order of instruments playing the *Allegro molto* Fugue are in the:

☐ SAME order as played in the 13 Variations ☐ DIFFERENT order as played in the 13 Variations

MUSIC HISTORY - PYOTR ILYICH TCHAIKOVSKY and THE NUTCRACKER (SUGAR PLUM FAIRY)

Pyotr Ilyich Tchaikovsky (1840 - 1893) was an outstanding Russian composer, conductor and musician of the late-Romantic Era. Tchaikovsky began piano lessons at the age of 7. He studied music theory and composition, and eventually became Professor of Music Theory at the famous Moscow Conservatory. He also wrote a book called the "Guide to the Practical Study of Harmony". Tchaikovsky's music is well loved.

Tchaikovsky wrote operas and famous ballets including Swan Lake, Sleeping Beauty and his enchanting fairy tale ballet "The Nutcracker".

The Nutcracker is a two-act ballet about a young girl named Clara and her mischievous brother Fritz at the Stahlbaum family's Christmas Eve party.

Act 1: At the party, Clara receives a gift of a Nutcracker solider doll. Clara falls asleep and dreams that mice are scampering around the Christmas Tree.

Her dolls come to life and a battle occurs between the Nutcracker doll and the Mouse King. The Nutcracker soldier turns into a real Nutcracker Prince who takes Clara to his kingdom, The Land of the Sweets and the Sugar Plum Fairy.

In Act 2 - The instruments played in the Dance of the Sugar Plum Fairy are the Flute, Oboe, Cor Anglais, Clarinet, Bass Clarinet, Bassoon, Horn, Celesta and the string family. They create a dreamlike sound.

A Celesta is an orchestral percussion instrument that looks like a small piano.

A Celesta has a keyboard and a simplified piano action in which small felt hammers strike metal bars. This creates a magical sound like tiny bells, unlike the hammers of a piano which strike strings to create sound.

The delicate sounds of the Celesta (patented in 1886) beautifully describes the Sugar Plum Fairy.

Go to **GSGMUSIC.com** - For Easy Access to the music and videos of Tchaikovsky's ballet The Nutcracker.

1. Listen to The Nutcracker - Dance of the Sugar Plum Fairy and answer the questions below.

    a) Name the composer of the Dance of the Sugar Plum Fairy. _____

    b) Name the percussion keyboard instrument used to create the bell like sound. _____

    c) Circle if the number of different instruments used in this piece is: 2 or 4 or more.

    d) Circle if the violins are played: legato or pizzicato or both.

    e) Circle if the tempo of the Sugar Plum Fairy is: *Andantino* or *Allegro Molto Vivace* or both.

    f) Circle if the Dance of the Sugar Plum Fairy is in: Act 1 or Act 2 or both.

    g) Circle if the Dance of the Sugar Plum Fairy is by: Clara or The Sugar Plum Fairy or Flowers.

MUSIC APPRECIATION - THE NUTCRACKER (WALTZ of the FLOWERS)

Tchaikovsky's music reflected his deep passion for communicating his ideas through sound.

"Music is an incomparably more powerful means and is a subtler language for expressing the thousand different moments of the soul's moods." - Pyotr Ilyich Tchaikovsky

Tchaikovsky's The Nutcracker was based on a story by E.T.A. Hoffman.

Act 2: The Nutcracker Prince introduces Clara to the Queen of the Land of Sweets (the Sugar Plum Fairy), and the Prince's family.

A celebration of music and dance begins. Dances from different countries representing sweets are performed for Clara.

The celebration concludes with the climax of the ballet, the final movement of the suite, with the Waltz of the Flowers danced by beautiful flowers.

Tchaikovsky's Waltz of the Flowers is sophisticated and theatrical. He was the absolute master for writing countermelodies (a secondary melody played in counterpoint with the primary melody) and decorative figures (ornaments).

In Act 2 - The instruments played in the Waltz of the Flowers are the harp, then 4 French horns introducing the main theme, then the strings with a beautiful melody. They create a decorative sound for the waltz.

Go to **GSGMUSIC.com** - For Easy Access to the music and videos of Tchaikovsky's ballet The Nutcracker.

1. Listen to The Nutcracker - Waltz of the Flowers and answer the questions below.

    a) Name the composer of the Waltz of the Flowers. _____

    b) Name the string instrument used to create the opening measures of the piece. _____

    c) Circle if the number of beats per measure in this piece is: 2 or 3 or 4.

    d) Name the brass instrument played to introduce the main theme first. _____

    e) Circle if the tempo of the Waltz of the Flowers is: *Tempo di Valse* or *Adagio* or both.

    f) Circle if the Waltz of the Flowers is in: Act 1 or Act 2 or both.

    g) Circle if the Waltz of the Flowers is danced by: Clara or The Sugar Plum Fairy or Flowers.

2. One of the pieces from Act 1 is called "Waltz of the Snowflakes". Name one of the pieces from Act 2.

_____

MUSIC ACTIVITY - MUSICAL INSTRUMENTS - COLORING THE ORCHESTRA FAMILIES

Moving around the orchestra, color each group of instruments that belong to the SAME Family of Instruments with the SAME crayon color.

So-La Says: Have Fun! Pick a color that you feel matches the Tone Color (Timbre) of each Family of Instruments! Write in the name of the color that you select for each Family of Instruments.

1. Color the Instruments of the String Family _____.

2. Color the Instruments of the Woodwind Family _____.

3. Color the Instruments of the Brass Family _____.

4. Color the Instruments of the Percussion Family _____.

5. Color the "Other" Instruments (that don't belong to a family) _____.

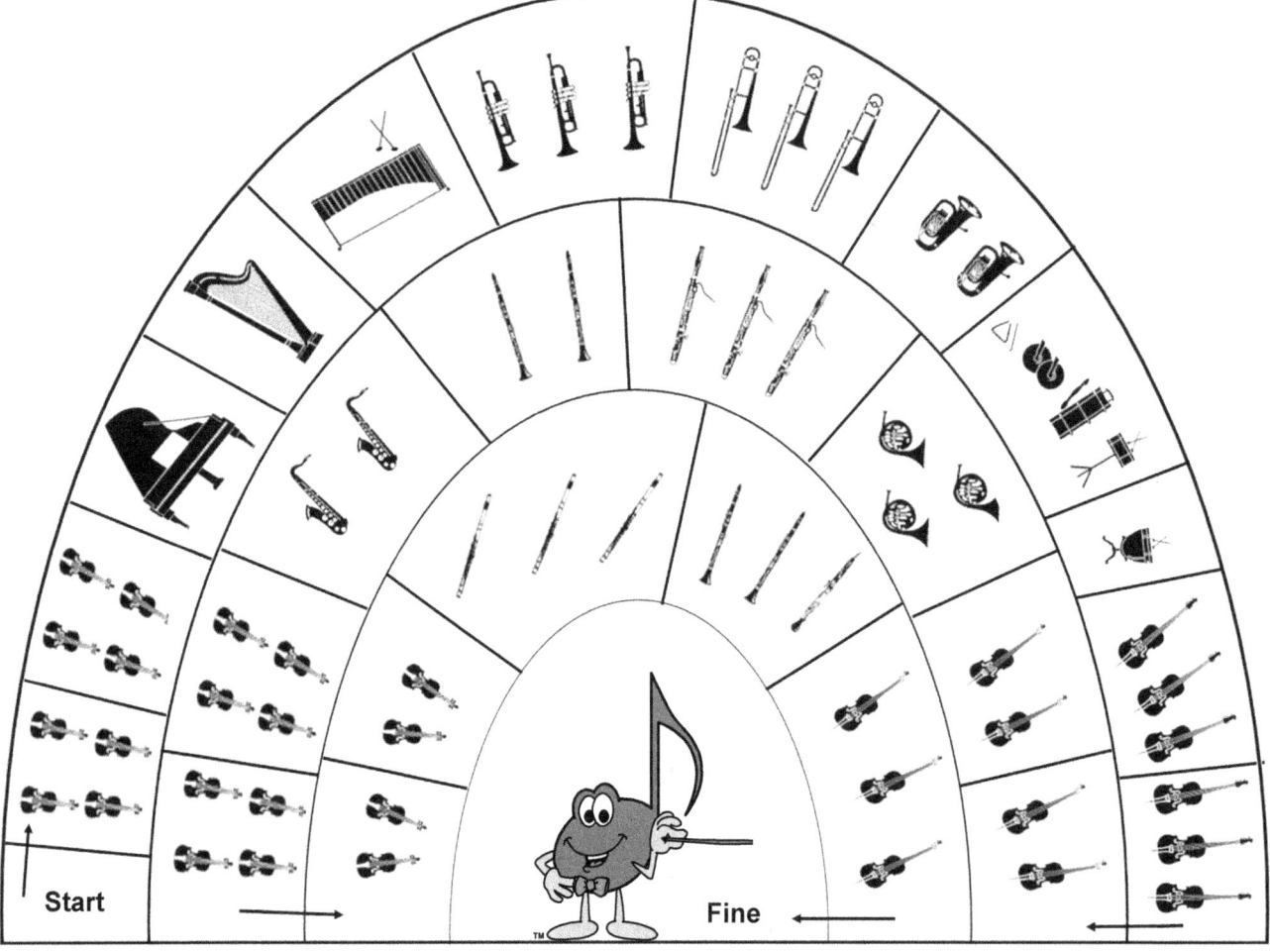

♪ Ti-Do Time: How many of the Instruments of the Orchestra can you name?

Discuss with your Teacher why you chose the colors that you selected to represent the Tone Color (Timbre) of each Orchestral Family.

Ultimate Music Theory
Level 4 Theory Exam

Total Score: ____ / 100

The Ultimate Music Theory™ Rudiments Workbooks, Supplemental Workbooks and Exams prepare students for successful completion of the Royal Conservatory of Music Theory Levels.

1. a) Name the Major key for each Key Signature.
   b) Identify the Scale Degree Name for each note.

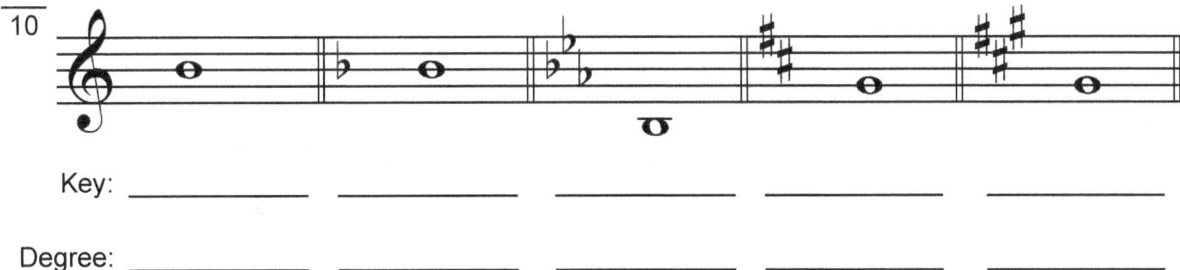

Key: _____ _____ _____ _____ _____

Degree: _____ _____ _____ _____ _____

2. a) Name the Major key.
   b) Transpose the melody down one octave in the Treble Clef.

Key: _____

   c) Name the minor key.
   d) Transpose the melody up one octave into the Treble Clef.

Key: _____

Ultimate Music Theory
Level 4 Theory Exam

3. a) Add the rest(s) below each bracket to complete each measure.

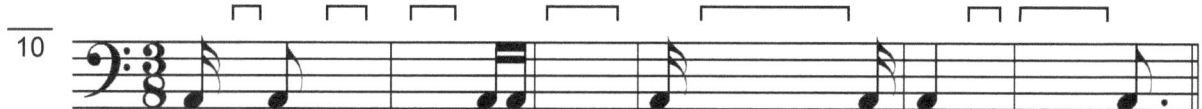

b) Add the correct Time Signature below each bracket.

c) Add the missing bar lines.

4. a) Write the following melodic intervals above each given note. Use whole notes. Use accidentals when necessary. Name both notes of the melodic interval.

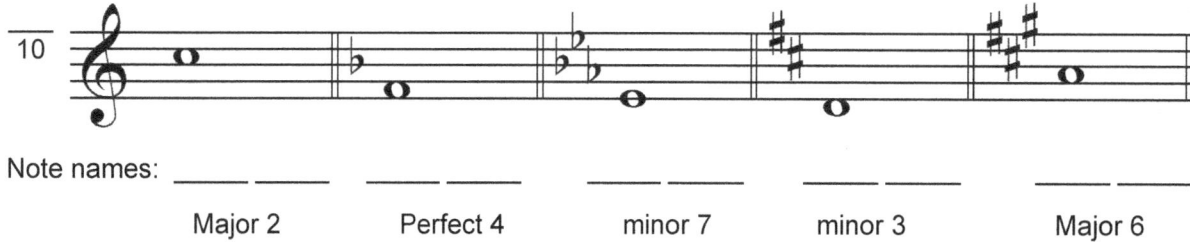

Note names: ____ ____   ____ ____   ____ ____   ____ ____   ____ ____

          Major 2   Perfect 4   minor 7   minor 3   Major 6

b) Name both notes (lower note first) of each harmonic interval. Name the harmonic intervals.

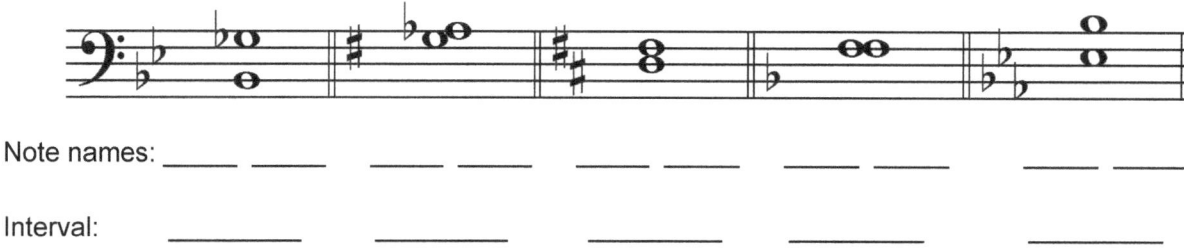

Note names: ____ ____   ____ ____   ____ ____   ____ ____   ____ ____

Interval: _____   _____   _____   _____   _____

Ultimate Music Theory
Level 4 Theory Exam

5. a) Name the Key.
    b) Write the Functional Chord Symbol below each triad (I, i, IV, iv, V).
    c) Write the Root/Quality Chord Symbol above each triad (C, Am).

___
10

Major key: _____   Relative minor key: _____

Major key: _____   Relative minor key: _____

Major key: _____   Relative minor key: _____

Major key: _____   Relative minor key: _____

Major key: _____   Relative minor key: _____

Ultimate Music Theory
Level 4 Theory Exam

6. Write the following scales, ascending and descending. Use a Key Signature and any necessary accidentals. Use whole notes.

__10__ a) A Major scale in the Treble Clef.

b) g minor melodic scale in the Treble Clef.

c) c minor natural scale in the Bass Clef.

d) f sharp minor harmonic scale in the Bass Clef.

e) E flat Major scale in the Treble Clef.

f) Fill in the blanks to identify each of the following scale degree names.

The scale degree name of the first note $\hat{1}$ of a scale is called the _____.

The scale degree name of the fourth note $\hat{4}$ of a scale is called the _____.

The scale degree name of the fifth note $\hat{5}$ of a scale is called the _____.

The seventh note $\hat{7}$ of a Major or harmonic minor scale is called the _____.

The seventh note $\hat{7}$ of a natural minor scale is called the _____.

Ultimate Music Theory
Level 4 Theory Exam

7. Complete the four measure melodies below. Observe the Key Signature and the Time Signature.

   a) Name the key.
   b) Use notes that move by repetition, step, skip or leap.
   c) Use the given rhythm. End on a stable degree $\hat{1}$ or $\hat{3}$.
   d) Draw a double bar line at the end of each four measure melody.

___
10

Key: _____

Key: _____

8. Match each musical term or sign with the English definition. (Not all definitions will be used.)

___
10

Term		Definition
arco	c	a) lively, brisk
prestissimo	___	b) *up bow,* play the note while drawing the bow upward
accelerando, accel.	___	c) resume bowing after a *pizzicato* passage
vivace	___	d) becoming louder
⊓	___	e) slow
mano destra, m.d.	___	f) as fast as possible
Tempo primo (Tempo 1)	___	g) left hand
'	___	h) becoming quicker
adagio	___	i) right hand
V	___	j) return to the original tempo
mano sinistra, m.s.	___	k) *breath mark,* take a breath (slight pause or lift)
		l) *down bow,* play the note while drawing the bow downward

Ultimate Music Theory
Level 4 Theory Exam

9. Complete the following questions by filling in the blanks.

   /10

   a) The composer of the "Young Person's Guide to the Orchestra" is _____.

   b) The 3 parts of the Young Person's Guide to the Orchestra are _____, _____ and _____.

   c) The composer of "Dance of the Sugar Plum Fairy" is _____.

   d) A percussion keyboard instrument that creates tiny bell like sounds is called a _____.

   e) Waltz of the Flowers is in Act _____ of The Nutcracker. It is danced by the _____.

   f) Each musical instrument produces a unique timbre called _____ _____.

   g) Each musical instrument and human voice has a lowest to highest pitch called its _____.

   h) The String instrument that plays the highest pitch is called the _____.

   i) The Brass instrument that plays the lowest pitch is called the _____.

   j) Name each instrument and its orchestra family as: string, woodwind, brass, percussion or other.

   Instrument Name: _____ _____ _____ _____ _____
   Orchestra Family: _____ _____ _____ _____ _____

   Instrument Name: _____ _____ _____ _____ _____
   Orchestra Family: _____ _____ _____ _____ _____

Ultimate Music Theory
Level 4 Theory Exam

10. Analyze the following piece of music by answering the questions below.

Waltz of the Flowers

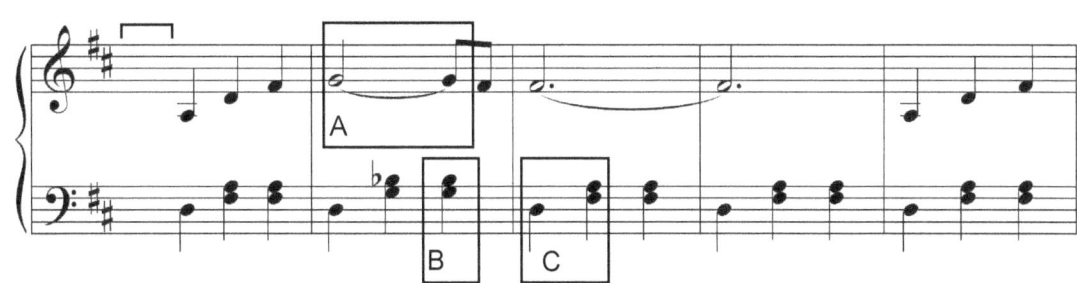

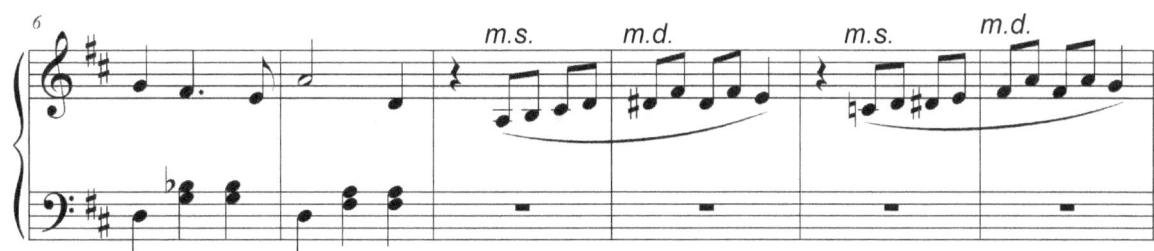

a) Add the correct Time Signature directly below the bracket.

b) Circle if the music starts on: an upbeat   or   a downbeat   or   an anacrusis.

c) Name the note at the letter A. _____   Give the total time value of the tied notes. _____

d) Identify the interval at the letter B. _____   Circle if this interval is: melodic   or   harmonic.

e) Circle if the triad at letter C is the: Tonic   or   Subdominant   or   Dominant.   Name the root. _____

f) In measure 8 and 9, explain the signs: *m.s.* _____   *m.d.* _____

g) Circle if the melodic phrase in mm. 8 - 9 and mm. 10 - 11 are: same   or   similar   or   different.

h) Circle if the half step at the letter D is: chromatic   or   diatonic.   Name the notes. _____ _____

i) Circle if the melody ends on: stable degree $\hat{1}$ or   stable degree $\hat{3}$.   Name the final note. _____

j) At the letter E, identify the: Root/Quality Chord Symbol _____   Functional Chord Symbol _____

Bonus - Play "Waltz of the Flowers" on your instrument.

Ultimate Music Theory Certificate

_____

has successfully completed all the requirements of the

Music Theory Level 4

_____   _____
Music Teacher   *Date*

Enriching Lives Through Music Education

www.ingramcontent.com/pod-product-compliance
Lightning Source LLC
Chambersburg PA
CBHW080023130526
44591CB00036B/2587